THE POWER OF *Purpose* in *business*

BY RHYS THOMAS

How to Achieve Extraordinary Success
with the Rhys Method® Life Purpose Profile System

Copyright © 2017 A. Rhys Thomas, www.RhysThomasInstitute.com

All material herein is the express copyright of A. Rhys Thomas. 2017 by A. Rhys Thomas. All rights reserved.

This is a general copyright notice for all written material appearing in this transcript and copyright infringement is a violation of federal law and is subject to criminal and civil penalties. All material described and discussed herein is owned completely and totally by A. Rhys Thomas. No rights are given to anyone to utilize, copy, replace, distribute, publish, display, modify, or transfer this material in any shape or form. Forms include written, electronic, or any other conceivable format and all requests to share or to republish this material must be approved by A. Rhys Thomas.

The author is not engaged in rendering professional advice or services to the individual reader. The ideas, procedures, and suggestions contained in this book are not intended as a substitute for consulting with a therapist in relation to life purpose, or business professionals related to business function. The author shall not be liable or responsible for any loss or damage allegedly arising from any information or suggestion in this book.

While the author has made every effort to provide accurate Internet addresses at the time of publication, the author does not assume any responsibility for errors, or for changes that occur after publication.

DEDICATION

To my many amazing staff, students, and clients who have forever changed the way I do business. They taught me that business is not "work" when what you're doing serves your highest purpose and the deeper needs of your clients.

WHAT PEOPLE ARE SAYING

"After spending 20 years in the staffing industry, I've used the profile system to transform how I identify the best candidate for a job. Being able to identify people's profiles and then match them with a job that serves their life purpose has been so satisfying for me and my clients. Employees feel successful and fulfilled, while companies are thrilled to have cutting-edge, transformational methods applied to their hiring and retention process. If you are in the business world, this work will shift your paradigm. You will see the power of harnessing the energy in and around you to manifest business success—beginning with identifying your own business purpose, to recruiting, managing, and retaining a world class team and work environment!"

JOANNE MUEFFELMANN

"Learning about the profile system has helped me connect to my highest purpose, inside and out. In almost no time at all, I created my product, "Sacred Cow – The Holy Granola Experience," that is now selling beyond my dreams. Once you discover your purpose in life, you no longer need to chase it—it chases you."

MAUREEN MALONEY

ACKNOWLEDGEMENTS

I wish to thank my team of editors, artists, and organizers: Nancy Marriott at New Paradigm Writing and Editing Services, Rachel Dunham and her team at Your Brand Therapy, Lisa Tarrant at HelpMeLisa, Joanne Mueffelmann HR Specialist and Principal at La Luce Healing, without whom I would not have been able to share this wisdom with the world.

CONTENTS

9	FOREWORD *by Kurt A. Mueffelmann*
11	INTRODUCTION

LEVEL 1: *Get Clear About Your Purpose in Business & Life*

17	CHAPTER 1: *Your Big Why*
27	CHAPTER 2: *The Rhys Method® Life Purpose Profile System*
49	CHAPTER 3: *Identify Your Business Deliverable*
71	CHAPTER 4: *Choose Your Perfect Career or Business*

LEVEL 2: *Give Them What They Really Want*

87	CHAPTER 5: *The Secret to Having Happy Customers, Clients, and Co-Workers*
107	CHAPTER 6: *Coaching Magic with the Profiles*
117	CHAPTER 7. *Branding on Purpose: Match Your Message to Who You Are*

LEVEL 3: *Create A Purpose-Centered Culture at Work*

129	CHAPTER 8: *Hire on Purpose with the Profiles*
141	CHAPTER 9: *Manage and Motivate Your Staff for Great Performance*
159	CHAPTER 10: *Create a Healthy Culture at Work*
169	CONCLUSION: *Where to Start in Your Business or Workplace*

APPENDIX

172	A. CHART: *How to Quickly Read the Profile of Anyone You Do Business With*
182	B. WORK SHEET: *Quickly Read the Profile of Anyone You Do Business With*

ABOUT THE AUTHOR

186	RHYS THOMAS

www.RhysMethod.com | www.RhysThomasInstitute.com

FOREWORD

How do Bill Gates, Donald Trump, Tom Brady, and Mother Teresa all succeed to become world leaders in what they do? They all have such different types of personalities, strengths, and weaknesses, yet they all rose to the top.

For example, you'd think Tom Brady was a team player, always talking about Team #1 and the role that everyone has to play to succeed. Yet, in a recent interview, he labeled himself as an introvert/shadow lion. Not exactly the type of profile you'd expect from a five-time Super Bowl champion!

As a business person, how do you approach such diverse personalities, communicate effectively, or even negotiate while understanding the various types of leadership and everyday personalities?

As a 25-year technology CEO, and two-time winner of the Deloitte Technology Fast 500 award, I've had these same questions and thoughts when dealing with various people; whether it be the overly-aggressive salesperson, the prima donna technology developer, the detail-oriented finance accountant, the touchy-feely (and sometimes passive/aggressive) human resources director, and lawyers involved in procurement, contracts, and other matters. Each of them has a unique way of approaching and dealing with issues. If you relate to all of them in the same manner, you're only being effective with one and not doing such a great job with all the others.

Carry that one step further: how do you effectively deal with the real-world of pushy cab drivers, unsympathetic airline or hotel reservationists, or even your children and spouses?

My dear friend Rhys Thomas does a great job of breaking it down to the simplest forms of not only identifying the key descriptive profiles of people across all aspects of business (and life), but giving the guidance and strategies for how to deal with various personalities on a daily basis, including the good, bad and even the unknown.

Have fun with this book and life in general. In our business, it has become a fun challenge for my wife and I to look at and/or interact with the unique profile types across the globe and see if we come to the same conclusion in identifying which of the five purpose-driven profiles a person best embodies.

BTW: I'm a strong *Charismatic Leader-Charmer* with a secondary *Knowledgeable Achiever* and a hint of *Team Player*—just in case you were wondering! In this book, you'll come to understand that unique combination of characteristics and what it means to do business with someone like me and also with so many others in their uniqueness. But most important, you'll get to understand yourself, and how you best do business when you discover your own unique profile combination.

Read on and enjoy!

Kurt A. Mueffelmann

INTRODUCTION

What does it take to have *extraordinary success* in business? Success beyond the ordinary—success that deeply fulfills you, lasts a lifetime, and gives others what they really want to keep them coming back?

For that kind of success, it takes knowing your purpose in life—what you were born to do and what you are passionate about doing. With that self-awareness, you can tap into the energy and the courage it takes to turn your passion into the career or business you are most likely to succeed in.

This book lays out the path to that kind of success. It's a path for everyone—whether you're a "solo-preneur" launching a new business or a CEO looking to scale. Small business owners, C-level leaders, and key senior managers will be informed and empowered by an approach that is purpose-centered and includes the whole self.

This is not the approach most popular business courses and books offer. They tell you that success in business is a matter of profit and growth goals that are achievable through training and systems. Just find the right job or business niche where you can make money, or where others that you want to be like are making money, and go there. If you're turning a profit and business is expanding, or you're getting regular raises, you'll be successful and happy—*right?*

Wrong!

You may be happy in the short term, but regardless of how successful you become financially, if you're not doing what feeds your soul and driven by the purpose you were born to fulfill, you'll never be truly happy. More likely, you'll stick with a job or business for the security and be in denial you could be doing what you're really passionate about. Or you'll change jobs endlessly, seeking satisfaction through a trial and error approach. At best, you're headed for a lot of stress, getting trapped in a vicious cycle that wears you down and makes you numb over the years.

There is a better way, which is what *The Power of Purpose in Business* is all about. When you know beyond a doubt what your purpose is in life and how to share your unique gifts—and you discover that *first*, not *later*—you will be ahead of the game and eliminate years of stress and suffering from your life.

TRADITIONAL TRAINING HAS IT BACKWARDS

So why do most business schools and books teach that to be successful *first and foremost* you need discipline and a strong will? That may work—but only up to a point. They neglect to tell you that unless you are clear about who you are and what you have uniquely within yourself to give—*to begin with*—your success, in spite of your strong will and discipline, won't last.

Traditional approaches do make an attempt to help you find the career or business you are best suited for, but their behavioral-based assessment tools are outdated. Many of these tools were developed decades ago, such as the Myers-Briggs Type Indicator (MBTI) personality test, the Dominance, Influence, Steadiness and Compliance (DISC) personality test, even the Enneagram test, and they don't address the needs of the modern working person for purpose-led work. Further, those more traditional assessments refer back to behaviors conditioned from early childhood, and so reinforce who you think you should be—and have been trying to be—your whole life.

But your past self is the very thing that is not working and has led you to take the assessment in the first place. In short, the more traditional tests tell you how to get even better at being the person you are not!

Unfortunately, most business trainings offer little support for you to find what touches your heart and soul, fulfills you at the deepest level of self-knowledge, and keeps you happily and successfully occupied for your entire lifetime. Instead, the typical business training has it backwards, putting the cart before the horse.

Think of the "horse" as your unique life purpose—the one you were born to live, and the source of your fulfillment and happiness in life. The "cart" is your business, your career or job, even your life. As your purpose in life, the horse needs to always be out in front of the cart, leading the way for your business or work to reach its goals. The horse is the power and energy that pulls your cart forward, so you can live an extraordinarily successful life.

Horses pull, they don't push. Therefore, the cart can never come first. And further, as you'll learn in this book, every horse (life purpose) has a unique kind of cart (business/career/job) that it alone pulls and delivers best. Some "horses" are strong and can pull great weight, while others are fast and love to race. Still others are graceful and are best suited to pulling a romantic sleigh.

But when you put the cart before the horse, you choose a career or business that does not serve your deeper purpose, and as a result your horse must either drag a cart it's not suited to pull—or worse yet, push a cart it was meant to pull. We all know that "push" feeling. It's when you are constantly grinding away in a job or business you hate, forcing the effort but going nowhere fast.

Your only option seems to be to try even harder. But with a horse misplaced behind the cart, you can't see where you're going, and so your real talents are being wasted. You're not getting better every day—you're just getting more and more tired.

When you are caught in such a vicious cycle, you can never deliver on your purpose in life. When you try to figure out the business or career you think you should have before you figure out who you are, you're putting the cart before the horse—and the road you go down will always be one of exhausting trial and error.

Isn't it time to discover how your purpose in life ("horse") can align to the work ("cart") you do? If you, like so many, are in your third or fourth job, career or business, and still feel like something big is missing, you'll want to find out what kind of horse is best matched to drive your cart—and then what kind of cart your horse is best designed to pull for the quickest route to success.

I'll show you how this is possible with the *Rhys Method® Life Purpose Profile System*, an assessment tool I've designed that brings business and personal assessment into the 21st century by including not only your talents and skills, but also your unique energetic expression—your soul. It's only at that depth where you can truly know your purpose and follow the path that leads to enduring business success.

THREE LEVELS OF SUCCESS

Whether you are employed or self-employed, are an entrepreneur with a small office, work in middle management, or are a CEO or executive in a mid- to large-size company, making choices and taking actions that are in alignment with your life purpose is your path to financial and personal success.

To help you maneuver and address your specific business needs, challenges and interests, the material in this book is presented on three levels, each level building on the one before to show you how knowing your purpose can increase your chances for success in any capacity or field: sales or consulting, human resources or IT, social services, customer service, life coaching or teaching—anywhere you interact with and serve others.

Level 1, *Get Clear About Your Purpose in Business and Life,* is for anyone who wants to discover their unique business purpose, regardless of the position they hold. Do you want a career change, to start a new business, or re-invent a business to be more in alignment with your purpose and passion in life? What kind of career or business lets you give the gifts you alone were born to give? You'll learn about the tool that helps you discover all of this, the Rhys Method® Life Purpose Profile System, and how my system applies not only to your personal life but more specifically to doing business or finding your perfect career.

Level 2, *Give Customers, Clients, and Co-workers What They Really Want,* expands to include the people you encounter in your work or business, whether you are a self-employed freelancer or part of a team in a bigger business. Who are they and how can you give them what they really want for a relationship that endures and is profitable for all? You'll learn how best to close the sale, put the right person in the right job, and create marketing and branding that matches your business purpose. If you are a professional coach, you'll learn how your knowledge of your clients' individual profiles can help you get them results that keep them coming back.

Level 3, *Create A Purpose-Centered Culture at Work*, is for company owners, managers, and executives who want to build their team and get great performance from their staff. Here I offer more hands-on guidance for business people to meet specific challenges: how to successfully recruit, train, manage, and motivate staff, with attention to the positions you need to fill and how best to do that with the Profile System.

My message is simple: When your purpose in life is the foundation of your business, you choose work that makes you happy and at the same time helps others get what makes them happy to keep them coming back. Financial increase comes naturally—not as your only or even dominant goal, but in direct proportion to how much you are living your purpose and giving the unique gifts that are yours to give.

That is the path of extraordinary success and happiness.

So let's get started …

In Level 1, *Get Clear About Your Purpose in Business and Life*, you'll be introduced to the Rhys Method® Life Purpose Profile System and have a chance to take a brief Business Purpose Self-Assessment to determine your own, your co-workers', and customers' profiles.

But before I show you how to use the Profile System for yourself and for those you do business with, I want to introduce you to your *Big Why* in Chapter 1.

Get ready to discover what drives you and be able to tap into an unstoppable energy for your success in business and in life.

Level One

Get Clear About Your *Purpose in business & life*

Chapter One
Your Big Why

CHAPTER 1
YOUR BIG WHY

Ever wonder why some people have the energy and courage to carry out a dream that seem impossible to most? Think of Martin Luther King, Jr. He had a dream, but the truth is, his dream had him, driving him to fulfill what he knew was his mission. That passion fueled his every action—his speech, his choices, his relationship to society and to the world.

You don't have to be a MLK Jr. to have the courage and passion to live your dreams. What you do need is what he had: total clarity of purpose and a mission that is uniquely yours to deliver. Ask yourself: What am I passionate about that drives me in life and business, that is mine uniquely to give to others?

The answer to that question is your *Big Why*. From that clarity comes a passionate sense of mission, one that is impossible to access when the work you do is only solving the short-term problem of money and security.

Your Big Why has to do with the unique quality that has always been in you, even as a young child. For some, it's the sense of creativity in your thinking, for others, a feeling of warmth and love that's in everything you do. Or your Big Why relates to a desire to be part of a team and contribute to a greater cause, or to being a leader who inspires others, or to be someone able to see the big picture and achieve much in life.

These are the five core qualities of the profiles you'll be learning about in the Life Purpose Profile System; one of which describes you and is the missing piece to you knowing your Big Why. What you do in life has got to have the same energy, flavor, and rhythm as this deeper quality within you if you are to be fulfilled. Once you reconnect with that innate and very unique quality, then the career or business you are born to do will be clear before you, and nothing will stop you from following it.

The Chinese philosopher Lao Tzu wrote, "He who knows others is wise, but he who knows himself is enlightened." Your Big Why is like enlightenment. In the East, they say: *Before enlightenment—chop wood, carry water. After enlightenment—chop wood, carry water.* Which is to say your actions don't vary when you become enlightened, but your perspective does.

Knowing who you are alters your experience of daily tasks and routines. When you know what your Big Why is, daily problems don't run you down, but rather offer challenges that strengthen your commitment to the path you are on. When you are not sure why you do what you do, every problem looms large, and eventually their accumulation leaves you exhausted with nothing more to give.

LOSING AND RECONNECTING WITH YOUR BIG WHY

You are living your Big Why the moment you are born. It is your true nature, a quality of being that is uniquely yours. As an infant and young child, everything comes to you exactly the way it's supposed to, and you don't resist any of it. There's nothing you have to *do* except to just *be* who you are, and that's how you live your Big Why.

This awareness lasts until between the ages of three to seven when there is a battle of wills—you vs. your parents. Eventually your parents win, and no matter how much you rebel or comply, or are perfect and strong, loving and helpful, that original awareness changes through daily conditioning and memorization.

> *"In my many years of looking for my Big Why, I always imagined myself as a big circle, and next to me was a little circle that was my purpose in life. Somehow I needed to find that little circle and get it into my big circle. But all along, that little circle—my Big Why—was right here inside me!"*
>
> MAUREEN MALONEY

You start behaving in ways you aren't naturally choosing in order to fit in and get more love or attention than you got as your younger, authentic self. You become who you think you are supposed to be in hopes of getting that love and attention, or just coping with a difficult family situation through your childhood. By adulthood, who you are supposed to be becomes your reality, dictating the programmed way you try to be successful in your work and relationships. But it never fulfills you.

As you grow older, your sense of self and purpose increasingly intersects with the "outside world" of others, your parents, siblings, playmates, schoolmates, teachers, ministers, and the laws of society that control them. In the outside world, people don't believe that anything you dream of is possible. They want you to believe what they believe, which is that only some things are possible. Even though these people have never met anyone like you, they already have an opinion as to who you need to be and how you should behave. When you behave the way they want you to, you are "good" and get love and attention. When you don't, you are "bad" and get punished or rejected. Over time, you make sure you are more "good" than "bad" and begin to trade who you really are for who you are supposed to be.

By the time you're an adult, you've given up on who you really are, that special *quality of being* that you were born with and is the key to your Big Why.

We all give up on our Big Why, our innate purpose and passion in life, in order to get along. But giving up leaves its mark. Being disconnected from your Big Why slowly starts to chisel away at your self-esteem, even if you're successful in the kind of work you do. Successful people can have low self-esteem because they know deep down they are really faking it.

Then there is a moment in life, usually in your 30s or 40s, when that person people expect you to be can't hold it together any longer. You've done everything you're supposed to do, and still you're not happy.

This happened to me. As a child I was a dreamer, happiest when perched 90 feet up at the top of the backyard pine tree, far above everything going on below. But that young child who liked to think he was flying realized at eight or nine that his dreams were not going to work in the life he had to live. I soon learned that guys have to be tough and have it all together, so I gave up my dreams and started competing in sports at age eight. From then on, I lived my life trying to always be the person society and my parents thought I should be.

Knowing who I am and finding what kind of work makes me happy is something I came by the hard way. I was a success in one industry for more than 25 years, but success only filled my wallet, not my soul. Eventually, I had to face the reality: my career wasn't working, my marriage was falling apart, and I wasn't being a good parent to my two young boys. All the while, a pervasive feeling that something was missing in my life just wouldn't go away.

It was a turning point when I realized I was living a life of quiet desperation, being good at something I never felt deeply passionate about. Looking back, it's clear that I had lost my Big Why.

MY BIG WHY TURNING POINT

My background is in competitive tennis. I played competitively into my 20s, then ran a large athletic club focused on coaching top juniors. For 18 years, I was director of tennis at a prestigious country club, becoming a soughtafter spokesperson and speaker for the tennis industry.

During my 25-year tennis career, I taught thousands of tennis lessons, coached some amazing athletes, and worked with hundreds of large groups of women, men, children, and seniors. On the outside, I managed staff, facilities, groups, payroll, and budgets while working long hours, keeping my clients and board of trustees happy. But on the inside, I was in love with the idea that there was something deeper than what can be seen with the naked eye. I consumed books like *The Inner Game of Tennis*, *Golf In the Kingdom*, and the works of Deepak Chopra, Fritjof Capra, Tony Robbins, and Wayne Dyer. I practiced martial arts three to four times a week, learning the power of the invisible "chi" energy that resides in all of us and determines so many of our life choices.

My tennis teaching turned out to be the doorway for me to share my deeper message, but in my position at a top country club, I spent five hours doing administrative work for every hour I spent teaching. Over the years, I lost my spark and desire. I was trying to be somebody I wasn't and could never get used to being a working robot like so many other successful people I knew. They didn't question things—they just made the money and got gray hair. I was trying to achieve success as I understood it: the six-figure salary, the big house and family, the prestige of coaching winners and getting awards. But it never made me happy.

In spite of numerous health and relationship crises, it didn't dawn on me until I was in my late 30s that I was not happy in my career and business. Even though I was successful, I never felt like I was truly being myself. I realized that what I loved to do most was encouraging my students to excel in their innate gifts, so I decided to take my own coaching advice and explore my innate gifts.

At 38, I enrolled in an energy medicine school in search of the deeper purpose I knew my life was for but needing some guidance in finding it. Little did I know that in less than a year what I was learning would change everything about the way I did business, hired staff, and over time change every area of my life and health for the better. In the energy medicine program, I discovered a humbling and profound thing about myself: I had no idea who I truly was, even though I was almost 40 and had a successful career, family, and stable life—at least as it appeared.

The turning point for me came when I applied my energy medicine training to my work. I'd learned that to heal someone, you help them remember what it feels like to be whole and alive, not just physically but energetically as well. Then you show them the places in their life where they are holding back from living fully, where they are stuck or blocked. Holding back the natural flow of energy in your life, career, or body, results in the same thing for everyone— you get tired and sick, have relationship problems, and usually have no idea if you are in the right career. I was having all three.

It was then that I took a hard look at who I was striving to be, that high-achieving business person who created products, spoke professionally, and made a lot of money. Then I looked at what really made me happy, which is awakening people to their purpose in life, giving them the courage and skills to express that purpose, and showing them how to gain the energy to do it every day—as well as make a good living financially in the process.

Although both paths—the businessman path and the teacher of purpose path—had the end goal of being financially stable, I could see that a huge shift would have to occur if I were to actually live my purpose, not just be materially successful. I saw how the businessman path that works so well for those born to be achievers was never going to work for me and make me happy. With that realization, I felt liberated to start focusing on the work I loved to do in my life. I stopped putting the cart before the horse.

LIVING MY PURPOSE

Today, after applying the principles I will share with you in this book, I know my true life purpose is not to be an achievement-focused businessman, but rather a creative teacher and writer, and a spiritual guide for people. For me, finding creative solutions and teaching something new every day is what deeply drives me.

My business and money-making skills are still essential to my success, but not to my mission. Now I earn more than I ever did in my earlier career, wake up thrilled every day to both work and play (now the same!), and deliver a service and product that is far more valuable to both my clients and me.

My resume does not include The Wharton School of Business or any business degrees, but it does include the training I needed to live my life purpose successfully. My resume includes mystical experiences, teaching, coaching, speaking on stage to large groups, and a second-degree black belt in the martial arts. It includes choosing the wrong job more than once, choosing the wrong relationships more than once, being a workaholic, working through physical and emotional issues in my life, practicing energy medicine, and being inspired by great thinkers and teachers who have gone before me to be different and be proud of it.

Today I run an energy medicine school of my own, the Rhys Thomas Institute of Energy Medicine, that is highly successful in business terms, so I guess I *am* a business person. Just like you.

THINK ABOUT YOUR OWN CAREER OR BUSINESS…

Maybe you, too, have reached a point where you've become painfully aware of a disconnect between who you are and who you have to be for your work. Even though you are successful in external ways in your business, if what you are doing doesn't feel like what you've always wanted to do—what you've only dreamed of doing—then you'll have a devil of a time making that business a lifetime commitment.

It's what you learn about yourself in your life that gives you the ability to run an amazing business and be successful. None of my gifts fit the traditional mold expected of a successful executive, yet I've pulled all these different parts together to be uniquely me. The person I thought I was supposed to be would have done things in a more organized way, but instead I took the road less traveled, the one that weaves back and forth, and has shown me things I would never have known had I stuck with the plan a more rational person might have followed.

How much of your resume shows your actual training for your true success, and how much is just a reflection of what everyone else is doing in hopes of being successful? When you know your purpose, you won't need to take a course in it; you'll realize that your entire life has been training you for it. You just have to get out of your own way.

Many business people come into our programs at my school to learn how to be more successful or learn to enjoy more the success they do have. The first thing they confront is the unspoken rule that successful adults must make lots of money and have a great career, and should feel like a failure if they don't. Participants in our programs learn that what truly makes a person successful comes from finding their deeper quality within, knowing who they are, knowing what they love to do and doing it—that is what will bring anyone extraordinary success and energy at all levels.

And it starts with reconnecting to your *Big Why*.

NEXT...

In the next chapter, I'll introduce you to a tool I developed called the *Rhys Method® Life Purpose Profile System* that offers a profound awareness of who you are and what your purpose is in life. You'll learn about five kinds of profiles that people embody and show up in business. You'll be able to easily identify your own unique profile, as well as the profiles of your co-workers, customers, clients or anyone you meet or deal with in the business world or in life.

Learning how to identify your own profile and the profiles of those you work with solves one of the greatest mysteries in business: *How you can deliver what people really want to keep them coming back for life.*

Chapter Two
THE RHYS METHOD® LIFE PURPOSE PROFILE SYSTEM

How to Achieve Extraordinary Success with the Rhys Method® Life Purpose Profile System

CHAPTER 2
THE RHYS METHOD® LIFE PURPOSE PROFILE SYSTEM

Knowing your Big Why—the passion and purpose that feeds all you do in life—is the source of you having extraordinary success in your business, job, relationships, even your health and well-being. Discovering the life purpose of your business is no different.

No matter where you are in the work you do—vice president or mail room clerk—the inner/outer balance of *who you are* and *what you do* is essential for your own wellbeing and the health of the business. If you don't have your own business and you work within another organization (someone else's mission), you can still be congruent with your personal vision and mission. You can discover how the business you work for supports your mission and gift, then contribute your gifts to make that business better than it could be without you.

In this chapter, you'll have a chance to discover your business purpose through the *Rhys Method® Life Purpose Profile System* by taking a simple assessment designed to reveal who you are born to be and what you are born to do in your life and work.

THE LIFE PURPOSE PROFILES IN BUSINESS AND IN LIFE

The Rhys Method® Life Purpose Profile System brings a new kind of workability to the workplace, one that starts with you knowing yourself.

You are a unique individual, unlike anyone else. But your uniqueness is not based on your personality or psychological makeup and past behaviors alone. The system I've created helps you to understand yourself at a deeper level, including your soul and your highest aspirations. Not just in business, but in your life. Your business success and passion becomes a metaphor for your inner success and passion for living.

Using this tool, you can identify the unique gifts you were born with and the purpose those gifts are meant to fulfill. It also reveals your dark or defensive tendencies, those qualities you've rejected in yourself that then sneak out to sabotage your efforts unexpectedly when things are going great.

I've been teaching the Life Purpose Profile System for 15 years to empower people to live their authentic self in a way that fulfills them and fulfills their purpose. Nowhere is that empowerment more transformative than in the realm of the work they do, whether in their career, profession, business or daily job. When you know your purpose, you unleash energy, skill, even health that you never knew you had, and you start to fully enjoy what you are doing while being successful at it.

The Life Purpose Profile System is a perfect business tool because it is simple and easy to use in business management, sales, job hiring, and team building. No one needs to fill out extensive surveys or learn complicated labels, or is ever reduced or pigeonholed in a way that doesn't truly fit who they here. The Profiles can quickly reveal who a person is and what their unique strengths and deeper needs and desires are. The system makes it easy for anyone to know a person deeply at first meeting, as well as day after day, working with or for them.

THE FIVE KINDS OF PEOPLE IN THE WORLD — AND AT WORK

The Life Purpose Profile System is composed of five different profiles, each describing a unique set of positive qualities and negative defenses a person can embody, and each giving access to a world of purpose and action.

Five kinds of people are described by the five profiles in the system: the *Creative Idealist*, the *Emotional Intelligence Specialist*, the *Team Player*, the *Charismatic Leader-Charmer*, and the *Knowledgeable Achiever*, as summarized in the chart below. You will know them as the *creative people*, the *feeling people*, the *caretaking or supportive people*, the *people who are natural leaders*, and the *highly achieving people*.

We each embody a particular profile based on our body type, emotional capacity, mental acuity, and energetic makeup. Your profile not only reveals what you do well for work, but who you are in your deepest essence and what motivates you, as well as how in defensive mode you sabotage your own best efforts. In reality, each of us is a combination of all five profiles, but only one profile will be primary. A secondary profile will complement the primary profile, adding the "flavor" that makes your primary profile unique.

The Profile System can also help you understand other people, the ones likely to show up in your work or business that you must relate to as coworkers, customers and clients, staff or supervisors. The following profile descriptions portray not only the strengths (core qualities) of each profile, but the weaknesses (defenses) as well. As you read through them, try and identify people in your workplace that fit these descriptions, and then see if you can identify which profile best fits you. Later in this chapter, I'll give you a chance to take a Business Purpose Assessment to give you a more precise identification of your profile as related to work and business.

THE FIVE KINDS OF PEOPLE AT WORK: QUALITIES AND DEFENSES

- Creative Idealists/Thinkers
- Emotional Intelligence Specialists/Poor Me's
- Team Players/People Pleasers
- Charismatic Leader-Charmers/Enforcer-Seducers
- Knowledgeable Achievers/Rule Keepers

CREATIVE IDEALISTS

Creative Idealists are the creative people, the innovators who come up with new and often brilliant ideas for solving problems. You may notice they are not always able to pay attention and can't necessarily stay focused all the time. To get the same job done as another person, the Creative Idealist takes lots of breaks and has a snack, maybe wandering around to think about it for a while. Hours later, they will have completed a project someone else could do in an hour, but it's done in a way no one had thought of before. In defense, as ***Thinkers***, they suffer from analysis-paralysis and spin mentally in isolation rather than produce any tangible results.

WHO ARE THE CREATIVE IDEALISTS/ THINKERS AT WORK?

- The coaching client who has an enormous vision for benefiting humankind but can't seem to write that first chapter of her book or get the simplest project off the ground.
- The playful and highly creative artist who stays holed up in his studio, often ignoring his wife and kids.
- The consultant/healer who can plumb the secrets of the universe but sounds a little off his rocker when he starts to talk about his views.

EMOTIONAL INTELLIGENCE SPECIALISTS

Emotional Intelligence Specialists are the feelers, the quiet ones who sit back and don't get involved in conflicts at the office. But their gift is how they talk to clients and make them feel. They have an ability to gently talk to people one-on-one and help them make decisions from their need to be taken care of and loved. And when you've got people on your staff who make others feel heard and understood, you're going to have a successful business. In defense as *Poor Me's*, they tend to collapse emotionally and see themselves as victims rather than be proactive in any situation.

WHO ARE THE EMOTIONAL INTELLIGENCE SPECIALISTS/POOR ME'S AT WORK?

- The co-worker or colleague who is always surrounded by exquisite beauty in the work environment but has to order everything from catalogues because she can't stand to shop in crowds.
- The social worker who is moved to tears at the least mention of harming an animal or child.
- The secretary who can't stand up to any criticism and collapses when confronted for the slightest error.

TEAM PLAYERS

Team Players are the supportive people, the ones who thrive when they are part of a team. These are the people who always say, *Okay, I'll do this and I'll help with that, and let me help you with this.* They're known for their dedication and loyalty, and are the first to volunteer for extra work and the last to leave when the job is done. In defense as ***People Pleasers,*** they long to be appreciated and will quietly resent having to do more than others.

WHO ARE THE TEAM PLAYER/PEOPLE PLEASERS AT WORK?

- The co-worker who knocks on your office door with a hot cup of tea when you aren't feeling well, but won't let you do the same for him.
- The smiling secretary or clerk who always has something cheerful to say when you are interacting with them but then disappears for weeks on end due to illness.
- The loyal employee who stays late at night getting the job done when all others have gone home but secretly sulks and feels unappreciated and resentful.

CHARISMATIC LEADER-CHARMERS

Charismatic Leaders-Charmers are the leaders, the ones who tend to be volatile and inspiring. They're the ones who will jump up on stage, and suddenly everyone around them is motivated to do something. These are people who tend to take the lead positions, because they have the energy and dynamism to pull it off. They make things happen quickly and spontaneously, and motivate others to get the job done. In defense, as ***Enforcers-Seducers***, they can make others feel about an inch tall in three seconds when in a conflict with them.

WHO ARE THE CHARISMATIC LEADER-CHARMERS/ ENFORCER-SEDUCERS AT WORK?

- The business owner who always seems to be the center of attention but can't sustain a one-on-one relationship that allows anyone else to share the glory.
- Salesmen/women who love the game of sales and motivating others to buy whatever they are selling.
- CEOs who inspire others to join them in new and often risky ventures that have big pay out or total destruction.
- The life of the party who is always charming and dynamic.
- The controlling boss who demands utmost loyalty yet turns the tables for their advantage.
- The chronically unemployed who take no responsibility for their lives, forcing others or social services to take care of them.

KNOWLEDGEABLE ACHIEVERS

Knowledgeable Achievers are the achievers, the ones who are gracefully efficient and achievement-oriented. They see the big picture and can trouble shoot better than others, mentally built to succeed in a business, always on top of the schedule and on time for meetings and appointments, and excellent time managers. In defense, as ***Rule Keepers*** they can be extremely picky and critical of themselves and others, even when a project is just slightly over time or budget, but they always get more done in a day than everyone else.

WHO ARE THE KNOWLEDGEABLE ACHIEVERS / RULE KEEPERS AT WORK?

- The life coach, manager, or COO who helps others stay on track and reach their goals, but who sometimes gets bogged down in the details.
- Multi-taskers who may be training for their second triathlon of the year, running a Fortune 500 company, and simultaneously driving a fundraising campaign for blind children, but are never satisfied that what they do is good enough.
- Consultants who manage the bills and other business impeccably, freeing you to indulge your more creative pursuits, but are hyper-critical of how you spend your money and time.

WHICH PROFILE ARE YOU?

Your profile, in both its core and defensive qualities, is the foundation for understanding why you are here on the planet—your Big Why. It all starts with your purpose in life. Awakening to your primary and secondary profiles puts you on a path to mastery in your life and business, and enables you to get off the trial and error path.

An easy way to tell which of the five profiles you primarily embody is by asking this simple question: *What gives you joy at work?* Is it:

- Sharing Your Creative Vision and Dream? (Creative Idealist)
- Heart Connecting One-On-One? (Emotional Intelligence Specialist)
- Teaming Up or Partnering? (Team Player)
- Leading Outwardly, Inspiring Others? (Charismatic Leader-Charmer)
- Achieving Inwardly, Personal Best? (Knowledgeable Achiever)

If you want a more precise identification of your primary and secondary profiles, go to my website, http://rhysthomasinstitute.com, where you can take a questionnaire that will sort out your profile composition in detail, providing not only your core qualities but your defensive qualities as well. My book, *Discover Your Purpose*, will give you even more details on your profile; available at Amazon or from my website.

BUSINESS PROFILE SELF-ASSESSMENT

The *Business Profile Self-Assessment* is a tool designed to help you discover your profile in the context of the business or work you do. It not only helps you identify your own primary and secondary profile, but also helps you to know the people you work best with because you understand their strengths, and how to better understand and work with the people who challenge you.

Keep in mind that you have all five of the profile types within you, but two of them, your primary and secondary, will be stronger than the other three. Likewise, the ideal work situation contains people made up of all five profile types (depending on the business size, of course), so knowing *who you are* and *who they are*, and how you can best work together for success is the goal.

Following is a short questionnaire to get you started. For each of the items below, there are six responses, and for each response you'll see a 1—5 scale, going from weakest to strongest. Circle the number that best describes you for each response.

Score your responses in the box that follows. (Find a longer, more comprehensive *Business Profile Self-Assessment* on my website at www.RhysThomasInstitute.com.)

In my work environment, I ...

    A. Help co-workers find creative solutions to complex problems.

        1   2   3   4   5

    B. Help co-workers experience a more tranquil and caring environment.

        1   2   3   4   5

    C. Team up with and support my co-workers, and make sure we are all pulling in the same direction.

        1   2   3   4   5

    D. Inspire and lead co-workers to get the most out of every day's work.

        1   2   3   4   5

    E. Give co-workers exactly what they need to complete their tasks on time, on budget, and within specs.

        1   2   3   4   5

    F. Am really good at all of these.

        1   2   3   4   5

When I am working on a team and a decision needs to be made, I…

A. Often start with a brainstorming session to get the big picture. I find the details work themselves out.

    ○ 1   ○ 2   ○ 3   ○ 4   ○ 5

B. Like when everyone can feel their needs are part of the decision. I'd rather hold off on a decision until people feel comfortable with it.

    ○ 1   ○ 2   ○ 3   ○ 4   ○ 5

C. Wait my turn in the discussions, letting the leaders and thinkers talk and work most of it out. Then I have a much better idea as to how to support the process.

    ○ 1   ○ 2   ○ 3   ○ 4   ○ 5

D. Like to get the decision maker to come to a decision and move forward. I don't like "meeting" something to death; action is more important than perfection.

    ○ 1   ○ 2   ○ 3   ○ 4   ○ 5

E. Follow a step-by-step logical process to assess the facts, so we get it right and don't have to fix it later.

    ○ 1   ○ 2   ○ 3   ○ 4   ○ 5

F. Am really good at all of these.

    ○ 1   ○ 2   ○ 3   ○ 4   ○ 5

When someone disagrees with me at work, I…

   A. Get anxious and my head spins. I withdraw wondering why they don't understand me.

   ○ 1   ○ 2   ○ 3   ○ 4   ○ 5

   B. Feel hurt internally but tend not to say anything. I hate confrontation and usually surrender my position rather than argue.

   ○ 1   ○ 2   ○ 3   ○ 4   ○ 5

   C. Say something humorous and immediately question my own logic. I do tend to waffle when challenged because I never like to make anyone wrong.

   ○ 1   ○ 2   ○ 3   ○ 4   ○ 5

   D. Challenge their assumptions. I'm not afraid to disagree with anyone and find much is accomplished through negotiation. I make them prove to me why what they believe is better than what I believe.

   ○ 1   ○ 2   ○ 3   ○ 4   ○ 5

   E. I ask them to explain their thinking and then find the hole in their logic, helping them see the obvious element they were missing.

   ○ 1   ○ 2   ○ 3   ○ 4   ○ 5

   F. Am really good at all of these.

   ○ 1   ○ 2   ○ 3   ○ 4   ○ 5

When first looking at a work project, I like to…

A. Take the broad view and look at many options.

◯ 1 ◯ 2 ◯ 3 ◯ 4 ◯ 5

B. See how it will impact the lives of others.

◯ 1 ◯ 2 ◯ 3 ◯ 4 ◯ 5

C. Ask others who have done it before for advice.

◯ 1 ◯ 2 ◯ 3 ◯ 4 ◯ 5

D. Figure out right away what its chances of success are so I don't waste my time if it's not a winner.

◯ 1 ◯ 2 ◯ 3 ◯ 4 ◯ 5

E. Pull together all the facts and create a timeline for what needs to happen to make the project run smoothly.

◯ 1 ◯ 2 ◯ 3 ◯ 4 ◯ 5

F. All of these apply to me.

◯ 1 ◯ 2 ◯ 3 ◯ 4 ◯ 5

LEVEL ONE | CHAPTER TWO

The way I feel about detail work and data crunching is…

    A. I enjoy research and finding new ways to analyze data.

        ○ 1   ○ 2   ○ 3   ○ 4   ○ 5

    B. I am okay with detail work as long as it is not dehumanizing.

        ○ 1   ○ 2   ○ 3   ○ 4   ○ 5

    C. It is not my strength, but I know it needs to be done if we are going to serve more people in a better way.

        ○ 1   ○ 2   ○ 3   ○ 4   ○ 5

    D. Every edge I can have on the competition is worth whatever it takes to get it.

        ○ 1   ○ 2   ○ 3   ○ 4   ○ 5

    E. Any business that doesn't pay attention to detail and the data will not be in business for long.

        ○ 1   ○ 2   ○ 3   ○ 4   ○ 5

    F. All of these apply to me.

        ○ 1   ○ 2   ○ 3   ○ 4   ○ 5

How to Achieve Extraordinary Success with the Rhys Method® Life Purpose Profile System

I want to be involved in a business that...

    A. Has a creative vision.

        ○ 1   ○ 2   ○ 3   ○ 4   ○ 5

    B. Is human and heart-centered.

        ○ 1   ○ 2   ○ 3   ○ 4   ○ 5

    C. Really helps people.

        ○ 1   ○ 2   ○ 3   ○ 4   ○ 5

    D. Is a huge success.

        ○ 1   ○ 2   ○ 3   ○ 4   ○ 5

    E. Stands the test of time.

        ○ 1   ○ 2   ○ 3   ○ 4   ○ 5

    F. All of these apply to me.

        ○ 1   ○ 2   ○ 3   ○ 4   ○ 5

ADD UP THE NUMBERS FOR YOUR 1—5 SCORES:

For A in all items, what is your total number?

For B in all items, what is your total number?

For C in all items, what is your total number?

For D in all items, what is your total number?

For E in all items, what is your total number?

For F in all items, what is your total number?

NOW RANK YOUR RESPONSES.

First, for *your own profile identification:*

Which response has the *highest* total number?
    If A, your primary profile is Creative Idealist.
    If B, your primary profile is Emotional Intelligence Specialist.
    If C, your primary profile is Team Player.
    If D or F, your primary profile is Charismatic Leader-Charmer.
    If E, your primary profile is Knowledgeable Achiever.

Which response has the *second highest* total number?
    If A, your secondary profile is Creative Idealist.
    If B, your secondary profile is Emotional Intelligence Specialist.
    If C, your secondary profile is Team Player.
    If D or F, your secondary profile is Charismatic Leader-Charmer.
    If E, your secondary profile is Knowledgeable Achiever.

Now, for the *people you work with:*

Which responses has the *third highest* total number? This, along with the first and second (your primary and secondary) will give you the top three profiles of the people you work best with.

> If A, you work best with the Creative Idealist.
> If B, you work best with the Emotional Intelligence Specialist.
> If C, you work best with the Team Player.
> If D or F, you work best with the Charismatic Leader-Charmer.
> If E, you work best with the Knowledgeable Achiever.

Which responses have the *fourth* and *fifth highest* total number? This will tell you which profiles you have the hardest time working with or appreciating for their work—your greatest challenges.

> If A, your greatest challenge is the Creative Idealist.
> If B, your greatest challenge is the Emotional Intelligence Specialist.
> If C, your greatest challenge is the Team Player.
> If D or F, your greatest challenge is the Charismatic Leader-Charmer.
> If E, your greatest challenge is the Knowledgeable Achiever.

Now that you have identified your own profile, and the profiles of the people you work with, use the next page to summarize and evaluate your results.

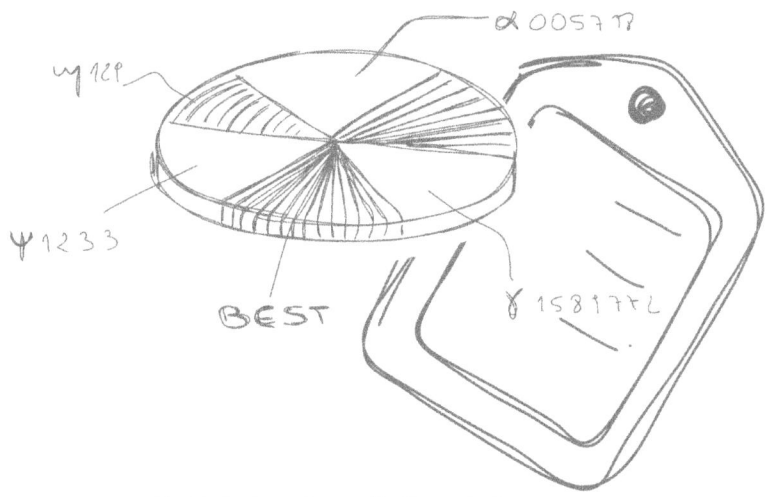

SUMMARY BOX

1. My Life Purpose Profile is (use 1 to indicate your primary profile and 2 for your secondary profile):

    Creative Idealist/Thinker

    Emotional Intelligence Specialist/Poor Me

    Team Player/People Pleaser

    Knowledgeable Achiever/Rule Keeper

    Charismatic Leader-Charmer/Enforcer-Seducer

2. The top three profiles of the people I work best with are (use numbers to indicate 1, 2, and 3; the first two will be your own primary and secondary profiles):

    Creative Idealist/Thinker

    Emotional Intelligence Specialist/Poor Me

    Team Player/People Pleaser

    Knowledgeable Achiever/Rule Keeper

    Charismatic Leader-Charmer/Enforcer-Seducer

3. The bottom two profiles I have the hardest time working with or appreciating for their work—my greatest challenges—are (use numbers to indicate 4 and 5):

    Creative Idealist/Thinker

    Emotional Intelligence Specialist/Poor Me

    Team Player/People Pleaser

    Knowledgeable Achiever/Rule Keeper

    Charismatic Leader-Charmer/Enforcer-Seducer

> *Mark this page for future reference,* so as you read throughout the book how the profiles function in terms of their deliverables, customer service, sales and marketing, and hiring and management, you will know how best to deal with them.

Later, I'll be telling you which profiles are best for which positions in a business, so if you are seeking to fill a position or seeking employment, you'll have a better understanding of who you're dealing with. Chapters 8, 9 and 10 go into greater detail about specific positions, and how you as a manager can benefit from knowing core and defensive qualities of any profile, as well as how best to relate to a person embodying that profile.

NANCY'S STORY: FINDING MY BIG WHY

In 2000, Nancy O'Keefe built a consulting company focused on helping small business owners. Over the years, her company became a virtual culture of 50 home-based employees in four states. Highly successful and in her early 60s, Nancy admits her business had become less than satisfying.

"It's fun to help people with the newest application, but I always felt something was missing," she commented. "As a child, I pictured myself on stage as a singer, playing my records in the basement and belting out show tunes."

As a student at my Institute of Energy Medicine, Nancy discovered that her profile is *Charismatic Leader-Charmer*. "So many things fell into place," she said. "I realized the business I was doing was really not making the kind of impact I had the potential to make."

That impact Nancy wanted to make gradually evolved out of her passion for helping small business owners into an entirely new venture. For some time, she'd been an advocate against domestic violence. You can hear the leadership quality of a Charismatic Leader-Charmer in her words: "As I started to think more about my life and what it was about, I realized that I wanted to be in a position to elevate women, to free them from being dependent on their spouses, and help them claim their earning power."

As a direct result of her first year in the school, Nancy began hosting a radio show for women, *Opportunity Knocks*, airing on E-women Network radio, about how to increase personal value in the market place. "I realized I needed a stage, and I needed to get out there to express my Big Why."

Following this realization, she joined a program to become a speaker and deliver talks about how women could become more assertive in the workplace. "Knowing who you are and what you're here to do is key to becoming assertive in any business," she said. "With the profiles, I'm able to quickly assess clients' profiles and encourage their strengths."

In the future, Nancy sees herself shifting out of business entirely and fully into the arena of women's empowerment, building up her coaching client business from her frequent speaking engagements. She is also leading programs for women through a new venture she's founded, Women's Leadership U, to help working women step into their value, earn what they are worth, and cultivate their leadership skills.

"My goal is to give more women the courage, the confidence, and the conviction to lead solutions to the problems we face every day in all areas of our lives and communities."

Spoken like a true Charismatic Leader-Charmer!

Chapter Three
Identify Your Business Deliverable

CHAPTER 3
IDENTIFY YOUR BUSINESS DELIVERABLE

The most important thing I teach people about being successful in business is that clients and customers don't come to you solely for your product or the service you offer—they come to you for *who you are*. They come because you inspire them, serve them, feed them, love them, guide them, or wake them up.

People can spend their money anywhere, but for loyal customers it's the intangible quality you bring to what you do that attracts most. This doesn't mean you can make a bad product or deliver poor service, and because you're a great person, expect people to buy. It means you have to match up the good products and services you offer with your own deepest purpose, and then deliver what is uniquely yours to deliver.

In each of the five Life Purpose Profiles, there is a common purpose that all your actions and abilities support. What you deliver within that common purpose is your unique gift to the world. When you deliver that unique gift to customers and clients, each one you relate to is left with a positive experience, regardless of what your business is about.

So what is your unique "deliverable" that wins you fans every time? In this chapter I offer you a brief self-inquiry exercise that helps you answer that question. But first, I want you to get how your gift is the thing you excel in above all else, something that you are born with and that you can discover through the Rhys Method® Life Purpose Profile System.

A sports metaphor for winning Olympic gold may be the best way to get my point across.

YOUR OLYMPIC GOLD MEDAL

What if your highest purpose in life was to win an Olympic gold medal in one specific event?

Well, it is. The only difference is that the events in your life are not track and field, skiing, gymnastics, swimming, etc., but rather the five profile core qualities: *creativity, emotional intelligence, teamwork, leadership,* and *mastery.* As in the Olympic games, each core quality contains individual events that you can excel at, demonstrating your unique gifts in art, poetry, healing, awakening others to their deeper self-esteem, having a successful business, creating new apps, counseling, being a comedian or actor, or a soldier.

If you wanted to win a gold medal in an event, your goal from the moment you were born would then be to figure out which one of the events you have a chance to win gold in, so you don't waste time on something that you'll never medal in and will never make you happy or fulfill your destiny. In short, knowing what your gift is—that thing you excel in—is the direct path to winning the gold.

But it doesn't usually work that way. Instead, we are told we can become anything we want to become and succeed in whatever that is—with hard work and discipline. But consider that is actually a lie told to you as a lie, one that sidetracks you for 30 to 40 years while you try to be who you are *supposed to be*, not *who you really are.*

The truth is that you were born to excel in one event and win the gold in that event year after year. It's only when you discover what that is will you be happy and find the vehicle (work or business) for sustaining that happiness. With that discovery, you realize you were born at the right time to the right parents, and with the right body, emotions, mind and spirit to deliver that amazing performance over and over again and get the gold every time.

Keep in mind that it takes anywhere from seven to nine years of five to 10 hours daily practice for most athletes to master their skills. The good news is that once you know who you are and begin to honor that throughout your day, then you, too, will be practicing your craft 5 to 10 hours a day—for a lifetime of mastery.

TAKE STOCK TO REVEAL YOUR GIFT

To go for your own unique gold, start by inquiring into your life. Look at the body you have (and include the body you've had at other times in your life for a general picture). What is your body perfectly designed for?

Can you see you have the perfect body for one thing? Picture the difference between gymnasts and swimmers—a gymnast's body is short and compact with muscles on muscle so they can flip and fly, while a swimmer's body is tall and thin with long arms and softer, more fluid muscles that glide through the water.

Now picture the swimmer on the balance beam and the gymnast swimming the butterfly in competition with the real athletes. Seems silly, but the truth is we are all given the perfect body to win gold in our event, and knowing your body type is the best pace to start. Are you thin like a creative person, soft like a feeling person, strong like a helper, dynamic and passionate like a leader, or balanced and in good shape like an achiever?

Now observe the energy your body carries as demonstrated by your emotions and nervous system. How sensitive are you? What have you always felt or been sensitive to? Notice that your mental capacity and what you focus on will be directly related to what you are sensitive to.

Lastly, go back to your childhood when you were in touch with your Big Why. What have you always wanted to be or do? What are the things you dreamt about that are different than what you do now? What are you deeply called to do now in your life?

Just knowing that your genetics and your inner callings are not random can give you power. To become congruent in both your business and your life message, you need to get clear on how all these aspects—physical, emotional, mental and in your deepest callings—are all related to your Big Why.

The ridiculous notion that we can dress for success is another way we try to be who we are not, hoping that the people looking at us are so shallow they only see our outer appearance. If you were to dress Michael Phelps, for example, in a leotard, he still couldn't flip around like a gymnast. How you dress and all the ways you brand your business have to reflect your unique gifts and talents, not something you are not.

Lastly, know that if the Olympic event you excel in is helping others to trust themselves more to excel in *their* Olympic event, that is what you deliver—your deliverable—in your business.

Here are five questions to start you on the path of knowing your unique gifts and having extraordinary success in business and life:

1. What kind of body, energy, emotions and mind do you have (not just now, but generally throughout your life)?

    - *Body.* Think about the Olympic event you have the perfect body for. Are you strong, muscular, flexible, super lean, tall or thin, shapely, square?

    _____

    _____

    - *Energy.* What is your energy like? Vibrant and outgoing, explosive, brooding, soft, enduring, low or lacking it, contained and focused?

    _____

    _____

    - *Emotions.* How sensitive and emotional are you? Super-sensitive to your environment, loving, thick-skinned, passionate, warm, enthusiastic, anxious, internal, dissociated, roller coaster?

    _____

    _____

    - *Mind.* What kind of mind do you have? Quick thinking, creative out of the box, practical, intuitive, emotional, socially thinking about others, organizational, dynamic, fearless…

    _____

    _____

2. What do you do for work? How are you currently using those qualities to make money, help and inspire others?

_____
_____
_____
_____
_____
_____
_____
_____
_____

3. Why do people come to you for your business? Why do they search you out and what do they want from you?

_____
_____
_____
_____
_____
_____
_____
_____
_____

4. After people work with you personally in your business, what changes for them, no matter how subtle? What would they say they got from their connection with you? Self-esteem, confidence, sense of freedom, a totally new outlook on life, awakened sense of humor, open heart, courage…

_____

_____

_____

_____

_____

_____

_____

_____

_____

5. Take your answer to #4 and put it into this sentence: I show people how to be more _____

_____

_____

and to feel more _____

_____

_____ ,

giving them the ability to _____

_____

_____ .

In sum, if you look back on all the people you've ever worked with, what intangible inner change did they walk away with after interacting with you? Your ability to define this is the cornerstone in building your business out.

Think of the successes you've had in your life, the people who truly benefited from doing business with you. That is what keeps customers coming back. You can have a great product, but if people don't connect with you, they will only buy from you for price and convenience.

SO WHAT IS THE UNIQUE GIFT YOU DELIVER? DO YOU HELP OTHERS TO:

- Open to their brilliance and awaken to more creative ways to succeed? (Creative Idealist)
- Feel a deeper, heart-centered connection to their mission in life? (Emotional Intelligence Specialist)
- Experience being supported, seen, and heard? (Team Player)
- Be uniquely inspired, impassioned or motivated? (Charismatic Leader-Charmer)
- See a more direct path to being successful? (Knowledgeable Achiever)

Exactly how you deliver one or more of these five gifts in your business or work may be a personal style issue, but in regards to your purpose in life, the gift you deliver is always the same in every area of your life. It doesn't matter what you are doing. And you being aware of how others change for the better after interacting with you or your business allows you to live your highest purpose.

Now let's take a deeper dive into how each of the five profiles delivers their unique gift to ensure customers and clients become fans for life.

YOUR UNIQUE PROFILE DELIVERABLE

Your business or work may provide a needed product or service to people, but their choice to spend their money with you is not only about your great product. It's about the "little" extra you deliver and often dismiss in value when you think, *Well, everyone does that...*

But not everyone does what you do. Each profile delivers their gift uniquely, and you can understand how you deliver yours—as well as how your co-workers deliver theirs—by reading the descriptions that follow:

CREATIVE IDEALIST

Your gift is to leave people with new ways of looking at things that they had never thought of before.

Body type and physical appearance: Your body, often tall and thin, can be childlike and nonthreatening in your demeanor. Your hair and clothes don't always behave or match, giving you a casual and fun appearance. You may find at the end of the day you are wearing two different colored socks and laugh.

You are irreverent, creative and funny. Your light approach to everything helps others access creativity in themselves that they can't access when they are with pragmatic people. Your natural ability to be open to higher wisdom in each moment lets you transcend limitations of the physical world and think outside the box most people live in.

When people walk away from an interaction with you, they often have a sense of expanded mind, sometimes even a little spacey but full of a sense of infinite possibility. They end up feeling like there is a creative way to move beyond their current impasse and start succeeding where they have failed before.

You have an ability to be above the general consensus of current-day thinking, which makes you a true innovator and often irreverent in what others get so serious about. This lets you help others

CREATIVE IDEALIST

overcome their mental or spiritual stagnation. You bring your genius, humor, and fresh perspective to others, and transform them into their highest level of consciousness. The mind is the tool through which humanity is becoming conscious, and you can help others take the leap and navigate that dimension.

IN THINKER DEFENSE, you will prefer to work alone, and tend to miss deadlines and meetings, saying, *Oh, was that appointment today?* Or, *Was I supposed to call you?* Even when on a team, you will somehow stop communicating. You often feel so scattered, you keep new ideas to yourself rather than be rejected for sharing them. You also avoid conflict at all cost and don't stand up for what you know should be done when faced with an aggressive client or boss.

WHEN PEOPLE RELATE TO YOU IN YOUR THINKER DEFENSE, they often experience confusion because what you're doing is too complicated to figure out. Thinkers seem distracted or dissociated, and their creativity may be lost in lofty ideals that have no grounding in reality. Or, if they are more scientific and mathematical in how they think, they are rigidly stuck in analytics when it's time to move forward on a project.

Keeping Creative Idealist customers, clients or staff out of Thinker defense is key to supporting their natural creative flow.

EMOTIONAL INTELLIGENCE SPECIALIST

Your gift is to leave people feeling heard and deeply cared for, no matter what the nature of your business may be.

Body type and physical appearance: Your deep eyes, rounded features, gentle touch, soft voice, and slow deliberate movements put people who are stressed at ease.

In the business world, where everyone must appear to be a perfect achiever and struggle with their inner critics, you are an oasis of compassion. Talking with you, people can let go of their stress for a moment. You see their heart, not what they are supposed to be or have done. Time seems to stop with you, since each feeling is not rushed and can be felt and moved through. This heart-centered place of compassion leaves people you work with feeling deeper self-love, and a soulful heart connection to their mission in life.

On a high ticket item sale, you are the one who helps them feel that the investment is in their happiness and that they are going to love it for a long time to come. You offer a view of a world in which each person feels that who they are is enough, just the way they are. They don't have to change and become someone they are not with you. They become aware and more confident in showing their more human and vulnerable side and that is what make their business and lives more real and accessible to others. Your ability to accept others unconditionally creates a wonderful environment for both clients and staff.

EMOTIONAL INTELLIGENCE SPECIALIST

You have a deep inner quiet that even if you don't feel it, others do, and they slow down, let go of their struggle and honor how much they love what they do and how they truly impact the world even when a specific event did not go as well as planned. Your natural compassion and empathy with people helps even the most guarded person come back into a level of inner peace.

IN POOR ME DEFENSE, you become overwhelmed by life and exhausted by relationships and work. This is where your deep ability to feel love and compassion for others shifts to feeling drained by them, and you blame and complain about people more than find moments of peace with them. Rather than having infinite patience for yourself and others, you feel you or they are not enough, and you feel bad, making it hard to show up energized every day.

You tend to need support from everyone in your life, more like a parent than a co-worker or coach. You either ask for it too often, complain you are not getting enough, or don't ask at all and just be down, all of which leads to other people rejecting or neglecting you. Your deeper connection with people is your life blood, and when you feel alone you don't function very well. You will say things like, *They should have known how that was going to make me feel*, or *Nobody cares about what I think*.

In defense, you have a very hard time in large group energy and tend not to say or contribute anything or avoid any part of work where there is a chance people will get upset. You may even cry or feel rejected when your boss gives you constructive criticism.

WHEN PEOPLE RELATE TO YOU IN YOUR POOR ME DEFENSE, they end up feeling you needed more help than they did, leaving them drained by the interaction. This is because you appear to be needy, constantly talking about your feelings with no intention of resolving them. They simply want to be heard for their pain, frustration or exhaustion, not offering any resolution.

Keeping Emotional Intelligence customers, clients or staff out of Poor Me defense is key to supporting them in their natural loving state that is so needed in the world.

TEAM PLAYER

Your gift is to make people feel supported and cared for in a direct and helpful way. Your deliverable gift is to help people be seen for who they are and know what they do is important, and that you stand behind them all the way.

Body type and physical appearance: You tend to be full-figured and warm, and give good hugs. You have a round face that beams when you see people, and you easily smile and laugh with them but never at them. Your eyes have an open or expectant look, always attentive to the needs of others. Your voice is jovial, and you love to listen more than talk. You have a strong back and can work tirelessly at a hard, physical job, like caretaking the elderly, as long as you feel you are doing them good. Your kind of body and energy make people feel safe and respected, and they immediately see you as a friend.

As a Team Player, it is your friendship and love for your family and friends that supports the entire underpinning of society. People's greatest need is to be seen, heard, and understood. You see each person truly and become a teacher for others to reach beyond the egoic self and share life with others. You offer the world a humble model for how to place the needs of others above the needs of the personal ego.

In business, your gift of supporting, cheerleading and validating others on their path to success translates to each person you work with walking away feeling better about themselves. Confidence must be earned in life, but you have a gift of reminding people that they have already earned the right to be confident in what they are doing and who they are. Your friendship comes first, even if you are doing

TEAM PLAYER

a business deal, so whomever you work with feels they have made a good friend.

You are a natural mediator for others in disagreements, because you can empathize with both parties and are therefore able to offer compassionate compromise. People who work with you in this regard feel they can work through even the most difficult negotiations and create win-wins in their lives.

IN DEFENSE AS THE PEOPLE PLEASER, too much caretaking, saying yes to everyone, neglecting yourself and feeling unappreciated leads to resentment that you do everything for others and they do nothing for you. This is where you shift from loving to help others and give great service in your business, to having to help others and feeling trapped in your work and relationships. Your constant conflict is this: Be helpful and have no life, or try to have a life and be a bad person who doesn't care or isn't doing enough to help others.

You tend to attract people over your lifetime who take advantage of your inability to say no and set boundaries with them, and they control you. Eventually, you feel like you just want to be alone, since no one in your life takes care of you, and you can't ask anyone to. You leave your job, get divorced or set out in your own business to "go it alone," but sadly you're never happy without people in your life.

WHEN PEOPLE RELATE TO YOU IN YOUR PEOPLE PLEASER DEFENSE, they'll get great service but won't feel the deeper connection and sense of friendship so present with a Team Player in their core. All goes well until you take on more work than you can actually do, and then start missing deadlines and getting stressed from trying to please everyone.

Or, since you have been doing everybody else's work for a long time with no appreciation, you start to passively resist. You say you'll do something, then not do it. You become resentful when others are upset that you didn't do what you said you'd do. People Pleasers never speak up until things have gotten really bad.

Keeping Team Player customers, clients or staff out of People Pleaser defense is key to supporting them to stay connected to people as the most important touch-point in any business for clients.

CHARISMATIC LEADER-CHARMER

Your gift is being able to inspire others to not only see something more in themselves but also take action on what they see.

Body type and physical appearance: Unlike the other profiles, Charismatic Leader-Charmers come in all shapes and sizes. You may have a penetrating gaze, be funny and charming with your words or loud and dominating, and have large shoulders and a thin waist (at some point in your life). You are often stunningly beautiful, and if not, you have interesting features that make you attractive and charming.

You have a high-energy charge, a quick-thinking mind, and a charm and confidence that makes people want to be around you. Each of these qualities makes you stand out in a room, and when you put attention on someone in the room that person will feel lucky and uniquely inspired or impassioned by the interaction.

You motivate others by finding what they desire most and showing them how to get it through your product or service or by following your path to success. This makes you the perfect salesman/woman or company leader, since people love to follow you and be around you, waiting for the magic to rub off.

When people walk away from working with you, they are inspired in some way and feel really good about themselves, as if you woke up a sleeping giant within them. They are uplifted and have a feeling that they can make massive change in their lives now, not later.

www.RhysMethod.com | www.RhysThomasInstitute.com

CHARISMATIC LEADER-CHARMER

If any of this is true for you, then likely all of it is true, and you just have to step into it more to experience it. Your charisma and passion become the energy and confidence others need in order to make changes in their lives. You become a role model for what it looks like to "go for it" in life and hold nothing back.

Finding your personal mission in life is the key to your success. From there you are able to call others to follow in your footsteps to find their own inner mission and cause that will inspire the world. You model leadership and fearlessness in what is often a jungle for the average person. Your ability to see the weakness and strength in an opponent in sports and at the right time exploit their weakness to win, is the same skill that lets you see the greatness in your clients and staff, and steer them away from their weakness towards their strength.

Once you work with someone, they feel a sense of direction and ability to navigate their lives in a more powerful and direct way. You unify groups of people to create positive change. No matter what you do, you carry the leadership energy to be a CEO of a business, a household, a sports team; and any group would be happy to have you.

IN ENFORCER-SEDUCER DEFENSE, you can use your huge energy against people or yourself. You can be bullying or manipulative or terribly self-destructive. When you are in this defense, people around you may look more like enemies, and you can't even trust yourself. You shift from outgoing and charismatic to controlling, angry, self-indulgent, and your use your power and charm to get others to do what you want with no real concern for it being good for them.

Since Charismatic Leader-Charmers always have at least some actor or actress in their makeup, their defense may be to play the role of one of the other profiles, such as feel depressed and overwhelmed like a Poor Me, or have anxiety and mental spinning like a Thinker, or be totally rigid and perfect like a Rule Keeper, or feel like a slave to their family and never say no like a People Pleaser. If this is true, when you're told you are a leader, you won't believe it, since you are really good at whatever role you're "hiding" in.

CHARISMATIC LEADER-CHARMER

Your mission in life is to make it to the top, but in defense you often burn bridges on your way up where success and money are your only value. This leaves you not able to trust people. You live in a dog-eat-dog world and are in hypervigilance all the time. You can't be genuine and vulnerable, so you play a tough or controlling leader role in your life relationships and work, rather than be real. You tend to be unable to manage your needs and desires, often overindulging in food, drinking, drugs, gambling, sex, fighting, cheating, etc. These behaviors can't help but affect your work, creating a shadow quality others sense that makes you seem untrustworthy.

In Enforcer-Seducer defense, you are rarely happy with what is going on in your work and not caring about how others feel about what you do. You prefer a battle to rationally working things out, since you know you can win a battle. This has you to incite conflict unconsciously and then blame others for starting it, even though you're always going to finish it.

WHEN PEOPLE RELATE TO YOU IN ENFORCER-SEDUCER DEFENSE, they find you refreshing at first because people love newness. But six months into the job, it becomes clear that you do not like to take direction, only to give it, and you will use any means necessary to get others to comply with your needs—not the other way around. You have a pattern of blowing up their work and your relationships every two to four years, never taking responsibility for your actions that led to the severance.

When relating to someone in Enforcer-Seducer defense, others can feel like they have been used or convinced or bullied into doing something they shouldn't have done. Or they feel cheated by some sleight of hand and not having been told the whole story.

Keeping Charismatic Leader-Charmer customers, clients or staff out of Enforcer-Seducer defense is key to supporting their natural power and ability as leaders to inspire others and close the deal.

KNOWLEDGEABLE ACHIEVER

Your gift is to help people find simple solutions to complex problems. You both educate people to be more efficient and create products or services that show people the most efficient way to get a task done.

Body type and physical appearance: You tend to be fit, trim, well-balanced and contained, sending the message that you have discipline and reserve. You appear well put together from your clothing to your hair and for women, your makeup. Your eyes look deep and are steady, always seeing a bigger picture of situations other get bogged down in with the minutia. Your appearance reflects your inner gifts of self-discipline, responsible authority, and an overall sense of wisdom.

You have a quick and calm mind, are always an expert in what you do often having worked many years in your industry and attained a high level of mastery in it.

You quickly assess people's skills, and may already use a profiling system to make sure everyone is in the "right" job. You also can see their deeper purpose, being a natural manager and business owner. No matter how much others have studied a subject, you have gone deeper in your own studies and are a resource in many ways to all the people you know. You can give sage-like advice and help people by guiding them on a project, then making suggestions for their personal life or health, which you are also expert in.

KNOWLEDGEABLE ACHIEVER

As a Knowledgeable Achiever, you are a natural in all forms of business. You innately understand the importance of delivering both an innovative product and doing it in an efficient and graceful way.

Your ability to see the big picture and influence others in a positive way and also your ability to have balance in your life is inspirational for those who are not as organized in their approach to life. After interacting with you, people come away with a clarity about their true abilities and how to begin the process of moving forward in their lives or businesses. Your ability to make what seems impossibly complex to the average person simple and understandable is your gift. The result is that you inspire and awaken in others the feeling that dreams can become a reality if they take them one step at a time.

Ultimately, you become the wise master people go to when they have lost their way in life. You may be the organizational guru that gets a failing business back on track or the experienced marriage therapist who survived your own divorce and has seen thousands of relationships turn around.

IN RULE KEEPER DEFENSE, too much analytical thinking and the judgment that goes with it, being a fixer of people's problems, and having a powerful inner critic creates a stiff and inflexible persona.

You may run your own business, work with a team, or be a supervisor or CEO of a large company but you have a hard time being happy because you always feel you could have done it better, and no matter how organized you are, things still fall through the cracks. This leaves you as a critical, exacting, workaholic boss to your staff and to yourself.

WHEN PEOPLE RELATE TO YOU IN RULE KEEPER DEFENSE, they find you are highly efficient and productive but shut down in your feelings, living almost completely in rational thinking which allows you to stay focused and get more work done. This makes you the perfect business "machine," but as a Rule Keeper, you are not happy, and others sense this.

KNOWLEDGEABLE ACHIEVER

Rule Keepers are the most rational of people to work with. You are great at making a meeting on time but terrible at thinking outside the box. In defense, your deliverable is a well-defined system, product or action plan but with no sense of the personal. If anything, other people feel criticized for being inept in whatever area they connect with you as the Rule Keeper.

Keeping Knowledgeable Achiever customers, clients or staff out of Rule Keeper defense is key to supporting their natural ability to organize and achieve at the human level and be less like machines.

NEXT...

By now, you probably can see that the Life Purpose Profile System can predict specific types of work and businesses a person will excel in. Once you know your profile, you can give yourself the best career and business advice ever, choosing work that fits your life purpose for a lifetime of success and fulfillment.

In the next chapter, I'll show you exactly what kind of job, career, or business is tailor-made for each of the profiles, so you can discover the best vehicle for delivering your unique gift. You'll also learn who might be best to work alongside you in the job, career or business you choose.

Chapter Four
CHOOSE YOUR PERFECT CAREER OR BUSINESS

CHAPTER 4
CHOOSE YOUR PERFECT CAREER OR BUSINESS

Success in life is easy when you have a clear foundation for what that success means to you. The work you do in life can only fulfill you when you connect the dots to find that no matter what you do, you're always delivering the same thing, which is you, your core or essential self. Whatever your choice of career or work is, if what you do is based on your unique gifts, it can't help but result in extraordinary success.

In this chapter, you will learn how each of the profiles fits best for different jobs and positions, careers and businesses.

Of course, you'll want to explore the best kind of work for your own profile. Then, think about others you work with. As a manager, is the job you are hiring for a good match for the applicant? If you are a coach, can you make suggestions within minutes of meeting your client on what they should do in their life or business to be happy and healthy for a lifetime?

Knowing what kind of work each of the profiles excels in can help you to discover the best vehicle for expressing your own life purpose and also guide you to help others in that same endeavor. Find your own profile in the section below, but be sure to read all five profile descriptions so you gain awareness of those you encounter as customers, clients and co-workers.

CAREER AND BUSINESS CHOICES BY PROFILE

CREATIVE IDEALIST

As a *Creative Idealist/Thinker,* you live more in your mind and in realms of infinite possibility than here on earth where the value of what you do is equated by a dollar amount. Therefore, the kinds of work you excel in are scientific fields, computers, mathematics, music, art, spiritual arts, and creative playfulness in life.

You may want to lead a business or team because no one else understands your mission, and the way you create any of the above fields will be totally unique to you. But if you do try to run your own business, be prepared for the long and winding road to success, not the direct route.

The direct route is not how your mind works. For the direct route, you will need a Knowledgeable Achiever employer or partner who can corral your brilliance and set a game plan. (The content of this book is being written by me as a Creative Idealist, but my editor Nancy Marriott is the Knowledgeable Achiever who outlines sections and chapters I can fill in, keeping me contained and on track!)

You are an idealist, which means as a scientist, artist, mathematician or spiritual guide, you are interested in only pure science, art, math and spirituality. You won't tend to be interested in spending your time on a corporate ad campaign, or doing business math that a calculator could do, or following a formula for creating pop music. You are a purist at heart and will never denigrate your ideas just to make money.

Even if you don't run your own business, you need a Knowledgeable Achiever business partner or business coach and investment consultant to help you stay on track and survive in the pragmatic world that you do not generally give much thought to.

You are best to stick to what you are good at, which is coming up with creative ideas that less creative people pay you well for. Trying to go it alone in the world of finance and negotiations will lead to much mental spinning and become a drain on your ability to be creative.

EMOTIONAL INTELLIGENCE SPECIALIST

As an *Emotional Intelligence Specialist/Poor Me*, you live more in your feelings than in your mind, and so you naturally connect to the world and people personally and with a caring heart. Therefore, the kinds of work you will excel in are healing or energy work, psychotherapy, teaching children or being a guidance counselor, working with the elderly or in hospice, or doing nonprofit work. You'll do well as a poet, writer, pastel artist, clothing designer, swim instructor—any kind of work that is done one-on-one.

Generally, you don't do well in a corporate environment because your purpose is to give the intangible, and you don't like putting a price on that. You do well in anything that helps others work through emotional issues to find a more gentle balance in their lives. You work exceptionally well in one-on-one interactions where you can give your client or staff member your total attention. You are the one who holds the heart and compassion in any business. Whatever form of work you choose, you bring a gentle touch that helps others feel seen, heard, and understood in ways they hadn't been aware of before talking with you.

If your work requires that you pay too close attention to details and rules rather than to others' feelings, you will hate it, and what you do to earn money will become a source of constant unhappiness.

TEAM PLAYER

As a *Team Player/People Pleaser*, you find your purpose in the people you are in relationship with. Helping them and being a vehicle for them to live better lives or achieve at a higher level is part and parcel with your life purpose. Therefore, you are happy in any line of work that serves others, such as social worker, massage therapist, psychological counselor, business consultant, or health attendant.

You are the smiling face behind the counter in the store, the social worker or nurse who treats everyone with love and integrity, the professional mediator resolving conflicts that are personal or legal, and being an advocate for those who need help. If there is a family business, you find your place in it, happily supporting it and enjoying the camaraderie. You are a worker at heart and rarely are without some kind of job. As long as the job has a family atmosphere where you can be supportive, you are happy doing just about anything.

You are the heartbeat of any organization, happy to do extra work if you feel it is supportive of the business and the staff. You love both your customers and the staff equally, and get any job done with a smile. You work well with others, even tough personality people. You don't demand the spotlight but are totally aware of your importance in any organization or group and in helping everyone on your team be successful.

The one job you are not cut out to do is being your own boss. You don't find it easy to make the decisions necessary to keep a business afloat, because your allegiance is solely to your clients. Team Player business owners aren't easily able to say no to clients, considering it disrespectful, and so they end up trying to be everything to everyone. A better choice is to go into business with a Charismatic Leader-Charmer or Knowledgeable Achiever partner who can handle tough money decisions.

CHARISMATIC LEADER-CHARMER

As a *Charismatic Leader-Charmer/Enforcer-Seducer*, you are naturally motivational and inspirational, using your deep ability to feel as a tool to sense the gifts of others and directly motivate them in each moment. Therefore, the kinds of work you will excel in are any area of leadership, sales, acting, security, always bringing your dynamism into whatever you do.

You have the energy to become a great athlete, actor, lawyer, law enforcement officer, soldier, politician, banker, stock broker, business executive, or consultant. Or you may be a social darling and influence others with your beauty and charm. You can be a powerful leader/manager who effectively takes charge of large projects and many employees, and you delegate effortlessly. Or you can be the strength behind the throne as Michelle Obama has been and lead as a partner to power.

You are a hero or heroine by nature. People want to follow you. Jobs such as fire fighter or soldier are natural to you, as well as being a champion of causes like women's rights, the environment, or the homeless. You often have a level of chaos and conflict in your life that others find overwhelming, but you thrive on negativity as a powerful motivator. You are so dynamic, others will ask you to lead their organization or group even when your life seems to be a mess. In business, you may enter a company and make it to the top faster than anyone else on the rise.

You know how to make money by offering products and services that are valuable and helpful to many, and you are not afraid of charging top dollar because you know your value.

KNOWLEDGEABLE ACHIEVER

As a ***Knowledgeable Achiever/Rule Keeper***, you are naturally organized and see the "big picture" of any situation at work and in life. Your ideas have both form and function, and you have a great eye for style and color. Therefore, you excel in almost any kind of work. Engineering, finance, COO, CEO, teacher, professor, scientist, nurse, doctor, lawyer, coach, consultant, mechanic, professional athlete, manager, human resources, banking, and on and on. Anything that challenges you both mentally and or physically, you will rise to meet it.

You are a fast learner, and if you are interested in making a business successful, you have all the tools. You will find the corporate world easy to navigate since you have all the skills they are looking for, which are discipline, intelligence, and the ability to work long hours and manage your time, still getting a golf or tennis game in at the end of the day.

You are an excellent long-range planner and can see the value of using money to make money. You invest in both your vision and through the current understanding of the market forces. Often you are more educated about your investments than your broker. You know that knowledge is the highest paid commodity in the world, and so you keep current in your own knowledge.

In your long-term view, you balance work with home life, both for yourself and for your employees. You are capable of working 24 hours a day when you choose to, but you are also just as likely to work the perfect nine-to-five workday and take regular vacations because you are efficient and get your work done quickly. The yoga and meditation courses you may be taking become a part of your general approach to life, not just as a means to de-stress after your work.

OH NO! DO I HAVE TO QUIT MY JOB TO LIVE MY PURPOSE?

People often ask me, *Now that I'm clear what I deliver and the work that supports me best, do I have to quit my job to be successful?*

No, you don't have to change your job, business, or profession in order to begin the process of living your life purpose. If you are good at your job and it pays well, stay with it, because there is one more important thing you need to do at that job before you leave. (If you are bad at your job and it doesn't pay well, you might as well leave now.)

The one more important thing you now need to do at your work is realize that you have no idea whether you like your work or not. You can't leave a job or a business until you get clear on this. And the only way to get clear on whether you like or dislike your job or business, and be absolutely sure it's not the one for you is this: For at least six months to a year, share your real gift—your business profile deliverable—that you've discovered in every way you possibly can, *in that job*.

In other words, be yourself for the first time in your job.

You see, once you actually bring your real self to work, others there might like you more, and then in turn, you might like them more. Being you, and loving being you, can be contagious, just like hating who you were at work was. This new person who brings his or her "A" game every day might find that the problem wasn't the job but rather the false person you dragged to work every day.

After just one year of every day showing up and sharing what you love to share, and asking for your real needs to be met from people on your staff, strangely you might actually begin to like your job and now know how to do it to fulfill your life purpose. If you find it's still not the right job, you have had a whole year of practicing what you'll be doing in your dream job, so you are totally clear what it will look like. No more trial and error!

SPEAKING FROM MY OWN EXPERIENCE

During the time I worked as a tennis director for a prestigious country club, I started my study of energy medicine and soon realized it wasn't my highest mission to coach country club people, run summer camps, and speak at tennis conventions. Once I discovered my deeper purpose of waking people up to their unique gifts in all areas of their lives, not just on the tennis court, I started thinking, *It's this job that's holding me back—What have I been doing with my life for the last 20 years?*

But as I was making plans to leave my job (and after over 20 years in the tennis industry I really had no idea where else to go), I was also applying the energy medicine knowledge of what I now call the Life Purpose Profile System to my staff, my clients, and my direct superiors.

Amazingly the job I was doing at the country club began to change. It started to be fun. I hired differently, I connected with the members differently. Furthermore, I had the stunning realization that I'd never actually been a tennis professional. I had been being who I thought a tennis professional should be and what the country club wanted me to be—not who I am.

Enlightenment comes in many forms in life. When I brought my real self to my job, it turned out that there was so much more I could do to make it enjoyable. I used the profiles to hire people who were born to do the jobs I needed them to do. To support my vision of what service really is, I connected deeper with the club members and had more fun with them as people, not just as paying clients I had to serve. I even changed how I presented myself to the board of directors.

I stayed in the job for four more years, and in that time I actually figured out how I liked to run a business and be in business, and what my real deliverable was beyond hitting a better backhand. Change was slow, but I had been stuck in my ways for a long time. Had I left my job at the country club when the light bulb first went on, I don't think the Rhys Thomas Institute of Energy Medicine would have become as successful a business as it is today. Building a business where everyone has a job they were born to do, and every client is seen through the lens of the profiles, I've found leads to happy employees and happy clients.

The truth is, back then, I didn't know who Rhys Thomas was, and I didn't know who my staff was that made my career work. I needed to apply the principles I'm sharing in this book before being fully ready to do business differently. That job helped me define who I was and who I wasn't.

Over time, I became the person I wanted to be. Of course, the board wanted me to be the fake person I used to be, and that was the deal-breaker. But I had used the job that I knew wasn't going to ultimately be my true, purpose-centered career to figure out how I could be happy and fulfilled doing business.

IT DOESN'T MATTER WHAT JOB YOU ARE IN

This was true for me and it is true for you. Your unique deliverable, your gift to give, is always the same, regardless of your position, career, or business you run. So stay in your job, just change who you bring to work every day. Then, when you have really done the job your way, you'll know if continuing to do that job can support your deepest purpose in life.

As you master how you love to do business in your current job, if that job is not your calling, you'll naturally be led to what is next for you. Or you'll get fired because your boss wants you to be someone you are not. Either way, you have an amazing opportunity in whatever kind of work you are doing right now to discover your purpose. Just apply the principles in this book and build your confidence in your ability to inspire others on your terms. It will be the best work you ever do!

My student Maureen Mann's story illustrates how knowing who you are can transform any work situation and give you a new career or business growing organically out of what you've always done.

> ## MAUREEN'S STORY: CHANGING FROM THE INSIDE OUT
>
> Maureen was an assistant principal in a high school when she discovered her purpose in life through the Life Purpose Profile System. Today she is a private practice therapist who blends traditional talk therapy with energy healing.
>
> "Before I came to accept who I am as an Emotional Intelligence Specialist, I lived through my secondary profile as a Knowledgeable Achiever," she recounted. "I was the ultimate Rule Keeper—rule developer and rule enforcer!"
>
> The Knowledgeable Achiever side of Maureen felt rewarded by her accomplishments, but it wasn't enough. She attended our program at the institute while she was still an assistant principal and got in touch with her more authentic self. Her experience changed how she experienced her job and ultimately led to a new career.
>
> "Knowing that I was really an Emotional Intelligence Specialist, I could still do my job, but I was now more emotionally present for students, parents, and staff."
>
> Knowing her profile and seeing how the profiles worked to help others had Maureen realize how much

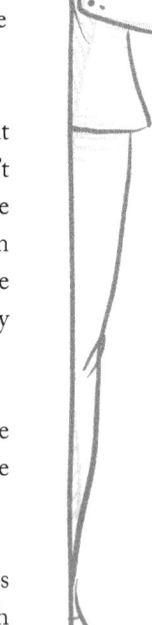

she wanted to do counseling full-time. Two years after she graduated from my energy medicine program, she left her job as assistant principal to start a new career as a therapist.

"In my new career, my relationship with my client is very important," she reported. "The compassionate, empathic space I'm able to provide—that's really what people need, so they can freely bring whatever they need to therapy. What allows them to grow is feeling heard and understood."

But Maureen did not leave her former job in the dust. "I still go back to my old school district once a week, knowing how underserved the mental health needs are for students in high school," she told me. "I counsel kids and do energy healing for them in school. My former colleagues see me, and sometimes they do a double take because I look so much happier. Some joke and say, *Stop looking so happy when you come here!*"

In her new profession, Maureen's Big Why is totally and completely fulfilled. "I love my job," she reports glowingly. "I have the privilege of meeting wonderful people and being part of their journey. It's such a gift!"

THE RIGHT JOB BUT THE WRONG CIRCUMSTANCES

In another scenario, you might be in the right job for fulfilling your life purpose, but because of circumstances, you can't fully express your gift and so are never fulfilled by what you're doing. That was the case for Sandra.

SANDRA'S STORY: DOING IT HER WAY

Sandra ran a large real estate company in Beverly Hills for many years, and every year she felt smaller and smaller. "I was literally shrinking, doing what I loved and what I had the skill to do, but the way I had to go about it was the problem." She had to minimize her skills, keep her opinions to herself, and behave in order to fit into the corporate environment.

As a Charismatic Leader-Charmer, Sandra was in a leadership position at her company in Beverly Hills—the "right" job for her profile. But even though her job clearly played to her strengths, she was in a situation where she felt dominated by an equally strong boss. When Sandra's boss went away, Sandra excelled and made the company a ton of money.

Eventually Sandra left corporate America and formed her own real estate company where she could do things in ways that were meaningful to her. For example, she ordered pink office supplies, something she wanted to do just because she couldn't do it in her former position. She felt free to be goofy, silly, smart, and intellectual, no longer needing to stay inside a box that didn't fit her true self.

Of course, all Charismatic Leader-Charmers at some point need to embody that quality of independence and

> fun, and so often strike out on their own. But when a company sees the bottom line that you are attracting more business, they will put up with your pink office supplies. In fact, no one can ever really stop you from being who you are, because internally you are your own slave driver creating your own limitations. When you re-discover your purpose, you'll be able to express that childlike quality within you that is exuberant, motivating, and inspiring to you and others for lasting success.

NEXT…

At Level 2, the focus shifts from knowing yourself and your best choice of job, career or business, to knowing your customers, clients and staff. You'll see how the Life Purpose Profile System is a tool to provide the best service for a profitable, purpose-led business.

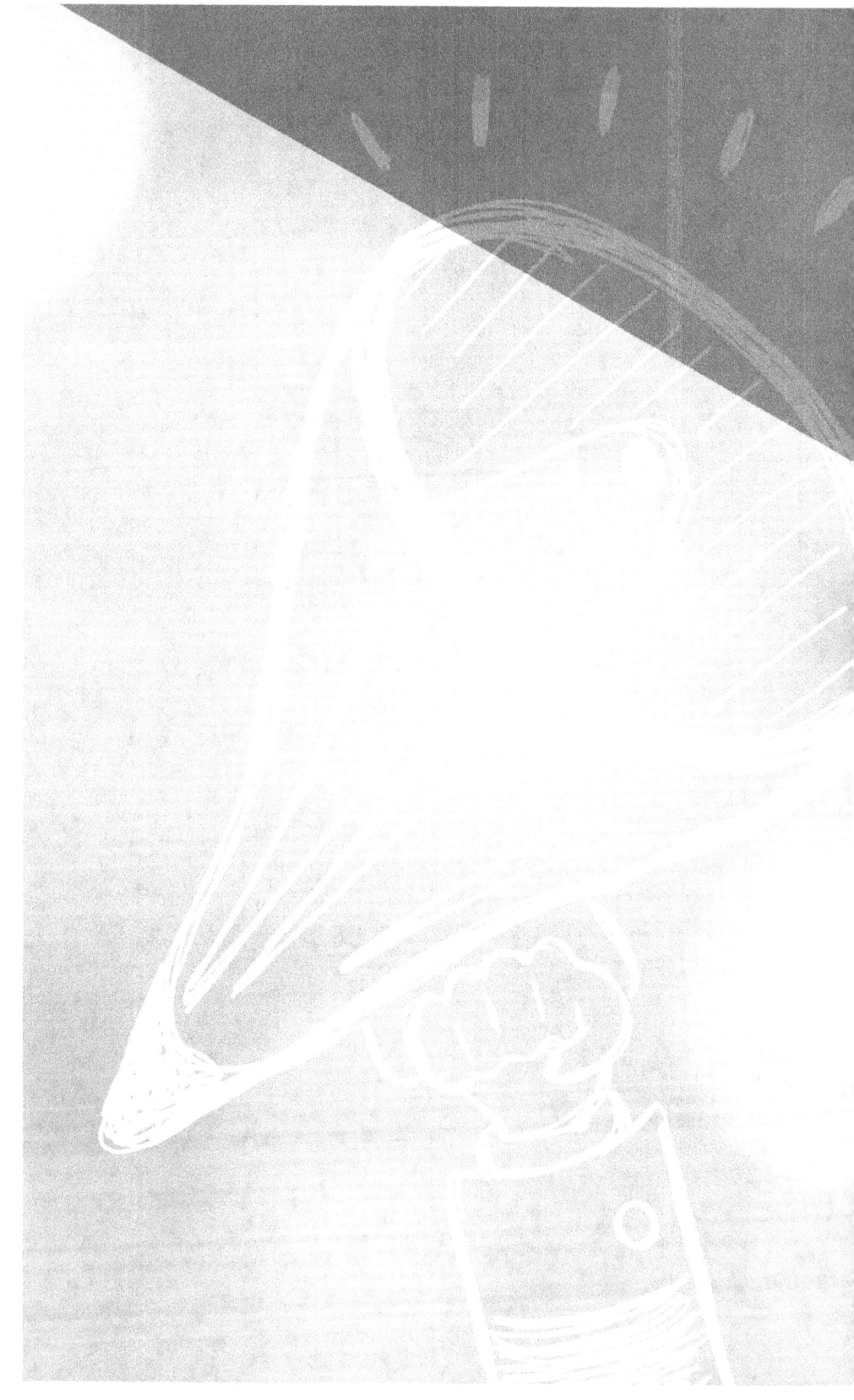

Level Two

Give Them What They *Really* want

Chapter Five
The Secret to Having Happy Customers, Clients & Co-Workers

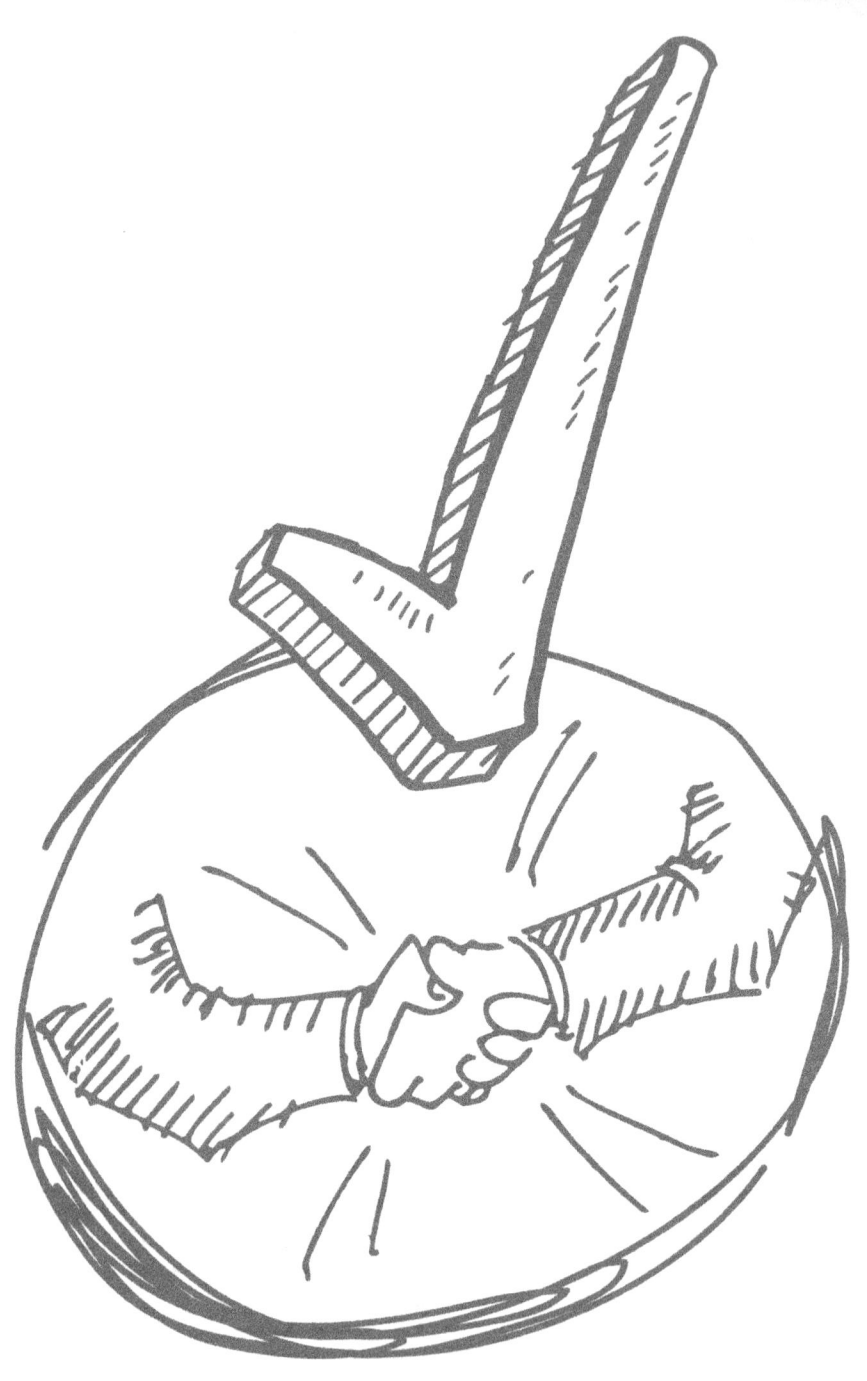

CHAPTER 5
THE SECRET TO HAVING HAPPY CUSTOMERS, CLIENTS AND CO-WORKERS

The secret to having happy customers, clients, and co-workers is simple: Give them what they *really* want. When someone comes into your business who isn't sure what they want, and you help them figure out what makes them happy, you have made a friend for life.

In this chapter, I will show you how you can give people what they want based on their profile descriptions. Each of the five profiles is unique in key areas for business: how people relate to money, how people are inspired and motivated, and how people are best communicated with.

Your awareness of each profiles' uniqueness enables you to tailor your approach for important business interactions. As a business owner, manager or consultant, you can save time and money when selling, consulting/teaching or hiring people by utilizing the Life Purpose Profile System.

Often a simple visual assessment is all you need to know a person's profile, based on the physical and energetic descriptions of each profile. (See chart in Appendix that helps you quickly visually assess your customer, client, or co-worker/potential hire.) Once you assess a person accurately, no matter what they may tell you they want, you'll know what truly makes them happy by understanding their unique needs.

FILLING UNIQUE NEEDS

Studies have shown that people buy products from certain businesses or work in certain jobs in order to resolve some kind of pain or stress they are experiencing in their lives, two to one over seeking more pleasure or happiness from their purchase. Therefore, what you offer a person in a product, service or job has to address their deeper need before they will even listen to you about the many wonderful benefits of your product or job.

The most pain and stress we all experience in life comes from not knowing who we are. When you don't know who you are, you'll always be second-guessing what to do, making hit-or-miss choices in your career, relationships, or health. It can be a rocky road, leading you to buy things that "everyone" *should* like but don't make you happy, take jobs that "everyone" *thinks* are good but don't fit your skills or temperament, or reject work that is in alignment with your true nature but is not "acceptable" in the eyes of others.

But your happiness doesn't come from the momentary success that others approve of or relate to. True happiness comes from having a sense of personal purpose over your lifetime that relates to the work you do, what you spend your money on, and what you do to make that money. And when you've found that, when your deeper need to know who you are is filled, pain and stress diminish.

Tailoring your service to the deeper needs of your customers and employees creates them being more loyal and productive. By using the Life Purpose Profile System, you can see what it is they truly need, and you can talk to them in their language so they know you know what that need is. If instead you're trying to make them perform and behave like you do or sell them the way you'd like to be sold to, you could be losing out on a lot of business. Not because you have a bad product, but because you aren't able to communicate skillfully with people in the four profiles that are not your own.

With the Profile System, you can respect the differences and honor the uniqueness of those you do business with, seeing them for who they truly are. This book may be about business, but knowing the Profile System can also help you in your personal relationships with children, friends, and family, and is just as important as when you are motivating or encouraging people in business.

Read on to learn how to tailor your services and communications according to customers', clients' and co-workers' unique qualities and needs, as represented by each of the five profiles in the Life Purpose Profile System.

KNOW WHO YOU'RE DEALING WITH AND GIVE THEM WHAT THEY WANT

Once you know what a person's profile is, you will have a wealth of information about them—more than ever appears on their resume/job application or is based on a "typical" customer profile. You'll know what's important to them, what specific pain or need you must resolve in order to succeed with them, and how to get their attention by speaking in a language they understand.

CREATIVE IDEALIST

CREATIVE IDEALIST/THINKERS are always looking for new and novel ways to improve their lives. It may be important for them to connect a spiritual purpose to the work they do, or to be meticulous in knowing the science and technology behind a product they are considering buying. Money is rarely their motivation, innovation is.

WHEN SELLING TO A CREATIVE IDEALIST OR CONSIDERING THEM FOR A POSITION, you need to talk to them about both the work they have done and the hobbies or side work they love. A Creative Idealist may be a computer programmer but also be in a band, while another makes *objects d' art*, enjoys meditation or Buddhism, or is part of some kind of new scientific research that is creating breakthroughs in healing or artificial intelligence.

You will need to inspire them with ideas, not products. They actually prefer the hypothetical but will have a hard time making decisions because they have so many options spinning around in their heads. Your goal with them is to focus them on something that gets them both the freedom they want (i.e., in a job), and is something that taps their natural creativity.

THE PAIN A CREATIVE IDEALIST HAS THAT YOU MUST RESOLVE FOR THEM is their level of anxiety regarding relationships and money. The anxiety causes them to spin in their minds with ideas that go nowhere, to avoid people, and to not be able to ask for what their work is worth or

CREATIVE IDEALIST

negotiate a living wage by using their creativity. The starving artist archetype is very common in the Creative Idealist. They are seekers in life, going from one thing to the next. Resolving their pain and helping them find a way to stick to one thing in their work while building a creative process around it can help them become more solid and stable.

If you are selling them a product or hiring them, the same holds true. Don't expect the Creative Idealist to be highly productive at work; they see the big picture but don't have the analytical mind that puts one foot in front of the other. As customers, you must capture their imagination and show them how cutting edge and new your product or service is.

TO GET THE CREATIVE IDEALIST'S ATTENTION, SPEAK TO THEM BY SAYING:

- *We are looking for someone who totally thinks outside the box.*
- *If you buy this, you'll solve…*
- *Do this one thing, and you can share your brilliance with…*

Keep the conversation light and let them change subjects as often as they want. Go with them but then bring them back to topic by saying, *Can you see how what you are talking about can integrate into this job (or product, etc.)?* If you see them as creative geniuses, artists, writers, poets, or mathematical savants, their anxiety will lessen.

Creative Idealists lead through innovation, and when you become a vehicle for them to express their innovative nature, they will be regular clients and motivated staff. They make great tech people and are at the heart of all new innovation in science and technology, art, and music. They almost always flop if they try to take their own ideas into the business market, since the business market mainly supports people with the profiles of Charismatic Leader-Charmer and Knowledgeable Achiever.

CREATIVE IDEALIST

As the idea person in business and not the execution person, the Creative Idealist must partner with others (Charismatic Leader-Charmers or Knowledgeable Achievers) to be successful. To bring out a new high-tech product or artwork never seen before, or to get a book published and read widely are accomplishments that take worldly skills they generally don't have.

When you see the creative idea person in a Creative Idealist and acknowledge that this is a gift they bring, you are well on your way to making the sale or hiring a great employee in the right position.

EMOTIONAL INTELLIGENCE SPECIALIST

EMOTIONAL INTELLIGENCE SPECIALIST/POOR ME'S tend to be quiet and nonintrusive. They want to feel that you care about them individually, and that whatever they buy from you will give them the ability to love and share more in their lives.

Money is rarely their motivation, while helping people through compassion and love is. Asking for what they are worth is difficult because Emotional Intelligence Specialists innately know that what they give is love, and it's hard for them to put a price on what comes naturally. They may reason, *If I ask for what I'm worth, then I'm just a heartless business person.*

WHEN SELLING TO AN EMOTIONAL INTELLIGENCE SPECIALIST OR CONSIDERING THEM FOR A POSITION, you need to talk to them about how your service or product can help them create a more loving and connected world for themselves and others. They may work as a therapist or a healer, or as a teacher of young children, or they may not have worked but raised their children and now feel like they'd like to have another kind of family to nurture. They also tend towards spirituality, yoga, and meditation in their free time.

EMOTIONAL INTELLIGENCE SPECIALIST

You will need to inspire them with a gentle caring that cannot be faked. They are highly sensitive and know immediately when someone is not being genuine with them. They buy from the heart and do not like to be pressured in any way. Decision-making is hard because they feel so deeply, and the feeling often takes over their decision-making process. With Emotional Intelligence Specialists as both clients and employees, you will need to gently keep them on task and remind them how much their loving presence does to support others.

THE PAIN THAT AN EMOTIONAL INTELLIGENCE SPECIALIST HAS THAT YOU MUST RESOLVE FOR THEM is their feeling of overwhelm that others deal with effortlessly. They tend to feel "less than" others, or not good or strong enough. They will often use the Thinker or Rule Keeper (Knowledgeable Achiever) defense to hide their pain and feelings, which in the long run causes even more pain for them. Their pain resolves when they see the real and lasting value their love and compassion creates in the minds and hearts of others.

In general, the business world does not value a sensitive and loving person, but a loving and sensitive person who is empowered to express their inner gifts on the team can buffer a competitive work environment, and instill compassion and caring. Emotional Intelligence Specialists help the other profiles slow down and smell the roses.

If you are selling them a product or hiring them, the same is true. Don't expect them to produce or buy rationally; they can get a job done and will buy, but not because it is the fastest way to go from point A to B. They will want to talk one-on-one about the real value of the work they do or the product they buy from you. Your ability to slow down and take time with them is the best strategy in both sales and work.

TO GET THE EMOTIONAL INTELLIGENCE SPECIALIST'S ATTENTION, SPEAK TO THEM BY SAYING:

- *Can you feel how this will really help others?*

EMOTIONAL INTELLIGENCE SPECIALIST

- *I think this is something you can wrap you heart around.*
- *This is specifically made to support empathic people.*
- *Caring and compassion are our highest values.*
- *Deep and meaningful relationships are essential for life.*
- *I love how sensitive and loving you are, and how you feel your decisions.*

Keep the conversation off world events or anything that can put them into emotional upset. Maintain eye contact and do not rush the talk or speak for them. If you have a position to fill on your team and know you have too many "get the job done" type employees, and you need someone who works more from the heart, take your time with them and see how they make you feel after talking with them one-on-one. That is their gift. The Emotional Intelligence Specialist is a dream to have on a team because they become the heartbeat of the team. In defense as the Poor Me, they can easily feel overwhelmed and take things personally that are just business to you.

If you are figuring out your new Emotional Intelligence Specialist client or student, take a deep breath before you try to fix them and get them "normalized" in some way. Often if they are in need of support, they are not looking for a solution, but rather want to talk about the situation and will improve when they feel better. Your tendency will be to jump in and help when they seem to be overwhelmed or going too slow. You can compress thinking but you cannot compress feelings. When you try to, the Emotional Intelligence Specialist becomes more stressed and goes into Poor Me defense.

When you see and honor the Emotional Intelligence Specialist as fearlessly willing to share their heart as compassionate teachers, poets, and lovers of all things beautiful, and helper of the little guy or the sick and infirmed, you will catch a glimpse of their true greatness.

They lead through emotions that so many others have shut down and need help in order to reawaken. When you become a vehicle for them to share that gift,

EMOTIONAL INTELLIGENCE SPECIALIST

they will become regular clients and motivated staff.

Emotional Intelligence Specialists make spectacular gentle and caring employees, volunteers, and yogis. But like the Creative Idealist, they are not focused on either money or structure, nor are they interested in being in charge. This means setting up and running a business without the help of a supportive Knowledgeable Achiever is unlikely and even partnering and being responsible for the daily operations of a business is not what they are here for. They are much better making the people who are here to run a business enjoy the process more. They will likely not work well with a Charismatic Leader-Charmer who tends to be more volatile at work.

When you see the Emotional Intelligence Specialist for who they really are, you know their deliverable will rarely make a blip on a profit-and-loss chart, but what they provide for people emotionally is priceless. Helping them see that gift as their power, not something for them to feel ashamed about, lets them feel at home in the work environment.

TEAM PLAYER

TEAM PLAYER/PEOPLE PLEASERS tend to be friendly, helpful, and hard working. They often have a tough time buying something for themselves but will spend all they have on members of their family. When they buy from you, they need to feel like you are with them on the purchase and afterward. In addition, if you can show them how good their purchase is, not just for them but also for the people in their lives, they will be very happy.

Team Players tend to be split on the value of money. They know they need to make it so they can take care of family and others, but they also have a hard time asking for what they are worth. A Team Player will provide a service out of the goodness of their heart, but once they have not charged for it, they can't go back and ask for payment. If you ask them why they give so much away to

TEAM PLAYER

people, they'll respond with, *They're like my family*, or *They were there for me when I needed help*. But because Team Players are so giving and nonconfrontational by nature, they cannot then change a deal or even raise their prices on old clients who have been loyal to them.

WHEN SELLING TO A TEAM PLAYER OR CONSIDERING THEM FOR A POSITION, you need to emphasize how your service or product can help them create an environment in their lives where everyone wins. As employees, they're often in the service profession and are excellent "first touch" people in a business. Team Players are not good sales people, but when someone comes in a business for the first time, Team Players are the ones that make them feel at home. They are equally as hospitable with other staff members and are invaluable on a team when it comes to lifting group morale. Giving them a position that isolates them from others never works and wastes their natural people skills.

You inspire Team Players by giving them suggestions as to what they can do better in their lives. They are excellent listeners and need your input to make any decisions for themselves. You and the people in their lives give them the feedback they need in order to please. This makes them terrible lawyers, since they want everyone to be treated equally and see the merits of the opposing plaintiffs case too easily. As sales people, they find a good reason to give products away at a much lower price. But they make great employees, since they are attentive, hard-working, good at following orders, and go out of their way to make sure the work gets done by the end of the day, even if they have to stay late.

Using statistics that show how many people buy your product and how happy those people are with it helps them make decisions. They never want to appear selfish, so decisions made that are for the good of all are easier for them than the decisions to do just for themselves alone.

TEAM PLAYER

THE PAIN THE TEAM PLAYER HAS THAT YOU MUST RESOLVE FOR THEM comes from their feeling of *I have to* rather than *I want to*. The Team Player by nature gives too much to others, offers more than they can deliver, refuses help when offered, and then feels resentful that others are disappointed in them or criticize their work rather than appreciate them. No matter how much they do, there is always someone they cannot get to, and they never want to let anyone down. Over time, they feel like they are the only one who cares in their relationships and work, and that no one respects them. This makes them pull away from people and become isolated, which is the opposite condition they need to fulfill their purpose in life.

Team Players need help letting go of certain people, relationships, or jobs that are taking advantage of their good nature, and then choose the service work they *want* to do, not *have* to do. To make this choice, they need to see the real value in what they do, but also to know their limitations and when to ask for help.

In general, the business world undervalues a person who is not an independent thinker, entrepreneurial by nature, and a tough negotiator. The Team Player is none of these, but like the Emotional Intelligence Specialist, they have a place in the world that is more caring, gentle, and humanistic, and may end up being more important to a business than the Knowledgeable Achievers and Charismatic Leader-Charmers who run them. If staff and clients aren't happy, there is no business.

TO GET THE TEAM PLAYER'S ATTENTION, SPEAK TO THEM BY SAYING:

- *This will be really good for everyone.*
- *This will make helping others even easier.*
- *I can see you care deeply about your work and the people in your life, but when do you get time for you?*
- *This product helps people who do too much have more time.*

TEAM PLAYER

- *Family comes first.*
- *This will make life so much more fun for your children.*

In an interview, keep the conversation in present time and about people. You can lead the conversation, and they will love to just listen, but make sure you turn it over to them to share what makes them happiest in life. Don't ask them what their goals are, because their only goal is to get through the interview or session. That is their gift—being here for you in present time.

When undefended, the Team Player is a dream to have on a team because they work well with everyone, and are warm and able to increase morale just by being themselves. When defended, as People Pleasers, they can be passive-resistant if they feel they are not appreciated for all the work they do.

If you are figuring out your new Team Player client or staff member, be careful not to ask them to do anything that falls outside of their expertise. They will always say yes but not always know how to do what you've asked them to do. They tend not to be the most organized or creative people, but when they are good at something and have been given specific guidelines, they will get it done with a smile. Make sure you do not ever force them to work alone on a project, or give them little feedback during the process. They are not comfortable in an independent leader role or in sales. They are leaders only in support.

When you see and honor the Team Player as caring and self-sacrificing in any service position from being your waiter in a restaurant, giving you a massage, working on your car, greeting you at reception, to running a bake sale for the children for a field trip in school, their purpose in life to serve and make the world a better place is fulfilled.

Team Players make spectacular friendly and caretaking employees, volunteers, and partners. But like the Emotional Intelligence Specialists, money is not the primary focus of their work, you are. Unlike the Emotional Intelligence Specialist, who will likely not work well with the strong personality of the Charismatic Leader-Charmer, the Team Player has much thicker skin and can

TEAM PLAYER

work well supporting the Charismatic Leader-Charmer or taking direction from the Knowledgeable Achiever. Basically, they work well with everyone but should not be put in charge. When setting up a business, such as a massage therapy practice, they should find either a Charismatic Leader-Charmer or a Knowledgeable Achiever to partner with who sees the huge value in their Team Player tendencies of hard work, and attracting and networking clients.

When you see Team Players for who they really are, you know their deliverable is a quality that makes people feel good about doing business with you or them. Helping them to see how much they care is empowering, not something to feel ashamed about, and will let their true gift support the happiness of many.

CHARISMATIC LEADER-CHARMER

CHARISMATIC LEADER - CHARMER/ENFORCER-SEDUCERS are constantly moving and growing, looking for the next big way to make more while working less. They like to make money fast or create a big change in whatever they are in charge of and then move on to the next thing. Showing how your product or idea can help them make a big difference now will be of most interest to them.

WHEN SELLING TO A CHARISMATIC LEADER-CHARMER OR CONSIDERING THEM FOR A POSITION, no matter what you're offering, you'll have to convince them that your product or service works for them as an individual. If you tell them that other people like it, they won't care. If you tell them it's a long-term strategy to their current problem, they'll fall asleep. You have to inspire a Charismatic Leader-Charmer to convince them to buy your product or join your team; they are passionate people and need to see how what you're offering is going to make something big happen in their life *now*.

THE PAIN THE CHARISMATIC LEADER-CHARMER HAS THAT YOU MUST RESOLVE FOR THEM is a combination of their urgency to make things happen, desire to not work for others or be told what to do, boredom

CHARISMATIC LEADER-CHARMER

with what they are doing, or chaos in their business caused by firing people or getting fired that now needs to be fixed. Because they are so dynamic by nature, life is filled with great highs and great lows. They won't need help for the highs but in the lows, they will look for solutions that others offer.

TO GET THE CHARISMATIC LEADER-CHARMER'S ATTENTION, SPEAK TO THEM BY SAYING:

- *With this, you'll make a killing.*
- *This will destroy your competition*
- *This will give you the edge you've been looking for, and it's totally invisible.*
- *This will make your business stand out and change everything forever.*

When relating to them verbally, let them lead the conversation and try to keep the whole discussion on them and their needs—their pain if they are a client or customer, and their skills and experience if they are staff. They are leaders and need you to see that in them, even if they are in denial of owning this quality. They need you to value their leadership style and how they inspire others.

You don't want to offer them a job or sell them a product that everyone else already accepts—Charismatic Leaders like to be the first. Even if you have a standard product or position you are filling, if you can show them how it uniquely works for them, you'll get better traction. Sales jobs and departmental leadership roles give them the freedom to lead in their own unique style. A product you provide with little or no effort required to use or something that has a fast learning curve is the best.

Charismatic Leader-Charmers make up 80 percent of the CEOs in the world. They love to start up companies or take over existing ones. They tend to be both charming, and simultaneously have hot tempers and be bull-headed. They will rise to the top fast in a company, or as business owners go from two employees to 50 in the blink of an eye, but their aggressive style can burn bridges along the way, leading them to lose trust in others and become isolated.

CHARISMATIC LEADER-CHARMER

Their *modus operandi* is to stay in one business for two to four years, then move on to the next conquest. They have to feel that their work is their mission. Helping them find their mission or being certain that you are in support of their current mission is essential when dealing with them. They are capable of staying with a business for many years, especially one they created, but they will still want to make major changes in it every two to four years.

When you see the leader and salesperson in the Charismatic Leader-Charmer and acknowledge that this is a gift they have, you are well on your way to making the sale or a having great employee in the right position.

When they embrace the Profile System, Charismatic Leader-Charmers quickly learn how to motivate and inspire others. Each profile has its own unique language, and when the Charismatic Leader-Charmer speaks all five of the profile languages, they can gain rapport and be successful in any situation.

KNOWLEDGEABLE ACHIEVER

KNOWLEDGEABLE ACHIEVER/RULE KEEPERS focus more on due diligence, structure, and organization than any of the other four profiles do. For this reason, if you're dealing with a Knowledgeable Achiever, you want them to see what you offer is going to be a long-term type of investment, one in which they're going to be able to see regular growth.

The Knowledgeable Achiever is more internally motivated than the other profiles. They are learners and are equally interested in acquiring new skill sets as in doing well in business or a job, both of which are the same to them. Your product or service must support them in a very organized, structured way, and if you can prove it does mathematically by providing statistics and facts, you'll more quickly gain their trust.

KNOWLEDGEABLE ACHIEVER

Knowledgeable Achiever customers are looking for the products or services that help them attain greater efficiency and production from themselves, from their product line, or from their staff. They don't want a quick fix because they know quick fixes never truly solve the problems. As staff, they often stay in a business or a position for many years because they love having mastery over their own lives.

WHEN SELLING TO A KNOWLEDGEABLE-ACHIEVER OR CONSIDERING THEM FOR A POSITION, be aware that they are always observing you to see if you are someone they can learn from. In other words, you gain their respect by being knowledgeable yourself. If they think you know less than they do, or you have typos in your presentation, or are not prepared to answer their questions, they will tend to walk away.

Like the Charismatic Leader-Charmers, Knowledgeable Achievers need to be related to as individuals with personal needs, but they also will be swayed to buy products or services by overall statistics showing how others have benefited as well. They will want to know how others have done the work you are asking them to do, or how others have used the product, both effectively and ineffectively. When you are talking to them for any transaction, it may seem like you need a checklist for what they deem is valuable so you can hit every one of the items on it.

THE PAIN THE KNOWLEDGEABLE ACHIEVER HAS THAT YOU MUST RESOLVE FOR THEM is their frustration and disappointment with outcome and performance. They can also get stuck in overworking by insisting on doing everything, which creates imbalance in their lives. This is frustrating because they place a high value on having balance in both their business and personal lives. Their weakness is that they are highly intelligent in analytical matters but have a hard time thinking outside the box. If you can give them tools to create more balance in any area of their life and help them see a bigger picture of their current situation, you'll do well with them.

KNOWLEDGEABLE ACHIEVER

TO GET THE KNOWLEDGEABLE ACHIEVER'S ATTENTION, SPEAK TO THEM BY SAYING:

- *Are you aware that studies have shown… (fill in the blank)…?*
- *Our research has shown that performance is enhanced in 70 percent of the people who…*
- *There is total tech support behind this product.*
- *The goal is nothing less than perfection.*
- *We are looking for someone who sees the big picture.*

In interviewing for staff, creating a conversation that lets them talk about their various areas of expertise puts them at ease and allows them to trust you. When you see them as knowledgeable, organized, skilled at what they do, and able to manage others, and you support them in being better at that as well as letting them make you more efficient, you will have their attention.

Regarding leadership positions, the Knowledgeable Achiever needs you to see that they lead by example, and their leadership style has the highest integrity. They inspire others to strive for a personal best, to be better every day in small and big ways. When you see and acknowledge that this is their gift, you are best able to hire them for the "perfect" job that they *really* want and need.

Knowledgeable Achievers make great COOs, managers, facilitators, teachers, trainers, and any position that requires detail work which they excel at. They can start up and run a business, and be successful, or enter any work environment to work their way to the top by playing by the rules.

Whether you are a business owner, manager, or consultant, you know it's all about getting your client or employee to perform well. But to perform well over the long-term, that person has to feel congruence between what they are doing and their deeper life purpose. Since most people have no idea what their real-life purpose is, your ability to support a person in finding this link, possibly for the first time in their life, goes far beyond simply helping someone find the right job or buy the right product.

Read about how my colleague Michelle put the profiles to work in her business.

MICHELLE'S STORY:
QUICK RAPPORT LEADS TO BUSINESS GROWTH

Michelle Thibeault is a physical therapist who has had a private practice clinic for 19 years. She treats patients specifically for pelvic floor problems, incontinence, and chronic pain management.

Learning about the profiles was a life-changer for Michelle. "First, it's allowed me to know myself, which has been a lifelong pursuit for me," she said, the first clue to her own profile as a Knowledgeable Achiever. "But it's also helped in my practice, especially when I do an intake evaluation and need to talk about intimate subjects. I need to establish rapport quickly, because I'm going to be asking them very personal questions."

Michelle treats her patients holistically, incorporating energy healing and dealing with their emotional lives as part of her treatment. "Being able to quickly assess what their profile is, I can talk to them in a way they understand. For example, I speak to Emotional Intelligence Specialists about their feelings and assure them that their strong feelings are okay. I give Knowledgeable Achievers the facts, explaining everything in detail. I let Charismatic Leader-Charmers know I see and hear them, that I'm paying attention to them, and I share ideas with the Creative Idealists and help them to get grounded. Team Players are easy, I just prescribe what to do, and they run with it."

Knowing how to relate to the defensive side of her patients' profiles is also helpful. "I can tell when someone isn't going to get better because they're not invested in getting better; for example, someone stuck in Poor Me (Emotional Intelligence Specialist) who can't get out of it. Or a strong Enforcer (Charismatic Leader-Charmer) who is using whatever they have to go against others. I'm always aware of the shadow side and can see where I can work with it or I can't."

Michelle has become skilled in the subtle variations of the Profile System and finds it to be a quick and easy tool that allows her to communicate smoothly and effectively.

"Being able to make a quick assessment with this simple tool has made my job so much less stressful and my clients so much more comfortable," she reports. "I know it's a key to the success of my practice, which has had a healthy growth rate over the years."

Chapter Six
COACHING MAGIC WITH THE PROFILES

CHAPTER 6
COACHING MAGIC WITH THE PROFILES

A relatively new industry is turning out tens of thousands of people to be coaches in business and personal growth. Before the advent of coaches, specialists in many fields were realizing that consulting was a great way to become an independent business owner and share their expertise. Now consulting has evolved into a profession that can benefit greatly from using the Life Purpose Profile System.

Whether you are a consultant or coach, knowing the Profile System gives you a distinct advantage in serving your clients. For example, when a client tells you they want to run a certain type of business, and you can see it's not in their nature or abilities as based on their profile, you're not only able to advise them against it but can offer them helpful suggestions as to what would work better for them.

You can also use the profiles to see a potential disaster headed your way, based on a client's defensive profile, and be able to nip it in the bud. You won't ever again get blindsided by the client who disappears in the middle of your work with them and never makes that final payment.

The following scenarios for each of the five profiles show how you as a coach or consultant can use the Life Purpose Profile System in your business to help clients be successful in their business goals.

PROFILE SCENARIOS

CREATIVE IDEALIST

A CREATIVE IDEALIST tells you his boss is thinking about upgrading him to becoming a manager because he is so creative and runs the software development team so well. You know from understanding the Profile System that Creative Idealists will never be good general managers of people in different areas of a business, so you advise him not to take the upgrade. Being a manager is not creative enough for Creative Idealists and will quickly take the fun out of working.

You might suggest that instead your client take a little more responsibility by offering to meet weekly with the new manager to brainstorm creative solutions to various problems, but leaving the software development team is not a good idea.

EMOTIONAL INTELLIGENCE SPECIALIST

An EMOTIONAL INTELLIGENCE SPECIALIST comes to you for help in controlling her emotions at work because she is too affected by having to fire people under her. You can see she has been stuck in Rule Keeper defense to avoid her deeper feelings, allowing her to do be tough and get the job done. But now her true nature is coming through, and the heartless way she's been going about firing people is causing much emotional turmoil that has her considering quitting.

You might show her that the key here is not in changing jobs, especially if she's really good at what she does. Rather, she could try bringing a different person (her Emotional Intelligence Specialist) to the job and discovering how a soft, compassionate person can let people go from positions that are not right for them, not just because they failed to hit their numbers.

TEAM PLAYER

A TEAM PLAYER seeks your coaching about setting herself up as an independent accountant. Because her dad was an independent accountant, she became a CPA, and she's thinking it's stable work that supported the family well when she was a child.

As an advisor or business coach, you would not support this.

> Instead you'd first advise her to take a job with a good local accounting firm or tax firm where she liked the people who work there. Then as a secondary possibility, have her talk to others in her CPA accounting classes who might want to partner in a business and find a good Knowledgeable Achiever if possible. You might even interview the person for her to be sure she is selecting a partner who fits the Knowledgeable Achiever profile.

CHARISMATIC LEADER-CHARMER

A CHARISMATIC LEADER-CHARMER tells you he wants to quit the sales job he's had over the last 15 years because it's been so volatile, so he can instead take a HR position at a big firm with more stability. You would have to advise him not to take it, knowing from his profile that he'll get bored dealing with people's problems and sabotage his success in that position within three to four years.

> You'd be better to advise him to find a position in a company where he can support that company's mission. He could then go to work for someone who is doing what he wants to do, help that person become even better at what they're doing, and ultimately offer to run a division within that company or create a similar business using a stable model.

KNOWLEDGEABLE ACHIEVER

A KNOWLEDGEABLE ACHIEVER seeks your advice on her plan to retire early at 55 from her 20-person business where she's been a workaholic, and focus on her tennis game to make the A-team at the club. You know that in Rule Keeper defense, the Knowledgeable Achiever will see the world as black or white, good or bad, and have trouble with shades of gray.

You remind her that she'll always want to be running or organizing something, and stepping back while still staying in the business, rather than out, is a better plan. Becoming compulsive about her tennis game is only replacing one compulsive behavior for another. Her tennis game does not create the balance she is seeking, but hiring an executive manager to run her business and slowing down a bit in her own capacity just might.

My colleague Margaret Lynch runs a personal development company that coaches people to become successful business coaches. An element of her training that sets her program apart from others is her use of the Life Purpose Profile System. By using the Profile System, she guides coaches towards what they will be most successful at and away from potential landmines. The coaches, in turn, have a tool to work with their own clients like seasoned pros in less than a year.

MARGARET'S STORY: COACHING WITH THE PROFILES TO NIP PROBLEMS IN THE BUD

Margaret always thought of herself as a person with the qualities of a Knowledgeable Achiever, having an engineering degree like her father and being a hard worker. She was shocked when she learned that her core qualities perfectly fit the profile of the Charismatic Leader-Charmer.

Knowing her true profile gave her a new and more effective way to run and build her coach training business. She learned that she didn't need to be the detail person, focusing on tasks that got her drained and exhausted, but instead could hire a Knowledgeable Achiever to do those tasks.

"As a Charismatic Leader, I get to do the things that are truly fun for me, and my energy and vibration are naturally at their highest levels," she affirmed.

In the personal development aspect of the coaching program she offers, Margaret uses the Emotional Freedom Technique (EFT), a clinically proven technique that consists of tapping on acupuncture points while voicing and experiencing intense emotions, anxiety, or the symptoms of PTSD. "With tapping, you voice and honor painful emotions, beliefs and self-talk, while effectively down-regulating the nervous system response to them, so they have less power over you and your life." she explained.

"So for coaches, the defenses of the profiles become a guide to navigating our clients' biggest blind spots and ways they may be denying their true gifts and greatness—even for people who've done years and years of personal development work.

"The greatest challenge in any coaching business is getting people to perform at their best, and a big part of that is addressing and clearing all the ways they stop themselves from making progress. This would be by isolating themselves, becoming overwhelmed, going into their inner critic, becoming guilty or ashamed when they make progress and going into battle with themselves, their clients, and even their coach. Being able to know how clients and even staff will self-sabotage themselves in advance can keep you ahead of such problems so you can nip them in the bud.

"If you have ever been blindsided by either a customer or an employee, where all of a sudden there's a subversive or negative thing happening, and you have no idea how to handle it, you know how awful that can be," Margaret said.

What she's talking about is every coach's nightmare: "The Rule Keepers give you a list of expectations they had but did not get met. The Enforcer-Seducers go into battle with you as an authority, or they spiral and self-sabotage, blaming themselves for their failures and then try to break their contract at exactly the moment when they need support the most. But if you can show these clients the way out of their self-sabotaging patterns, they will be forever grateful."

Margaret recommends that her coaches communicate

> skillfully with people in each of the profiles when they get out of their comfort zone, become scared, and self-sabotage uniquely in the way their profile says they will.
>
> "The ability to understand a client, instead of being in shock at how they are acting, allows coaches to respectfully honor the clients self-sabotage process and move them through it with presence and compassion. Clients are able to see clearly their most self-defeating patterns while experiencing caring support and the challenge to move forward. This often results in an email the next day, saying, *Thank you, no one's ever done that for me before... I'm so appreciative, and I'm so sorry about what I said.*"

Coaching Tip: Besides heading off landmines and nipping potential problems in the bud, the Profile System lets you focus on the innate greatness of your client, their positive core soul qualities, and support clients in strengthening those qualities as you coach them around their defenses.

Chapter Seven
Branding on Purpose: Match Your Message to Who You Are

CHAPTER 7
BRANDING ON PURPOSE: MATCH YOUR MESSAGE TO WHO YOU ARE

The Holy Grail of business is marketing and sales, and for you to have extraordinary success in both, your message has to be congruent with who you are.

I won't pretend that I'm an expert in either marketing or sales, but I can tell you for certain that to attract your perfect customer, your marketing message and brand must be congruent with your deeper purpose. Employing the standard marketing practices may get you results and overall improve your bottom line, but just like striving to be someone you're supposed to be, not who you truly are, it won't work in the long run.

What you have learned about yourself from reading the first six chapters of this book and discovering your own profile tells you what the unique *message* is that you deliver. Now, you will learn how to best get across your unique message through a marketing strategy specific to your profile.

YOUR PROFILE STYLE

Ask yourself: What's my strongest avenue for marketing my product or service? You may be great on video, or maybe better on Facebook or social media. You may know how to write great email copy, or be a "sound bite machine" on Twitter. Do you excel at face-to-face meetings and love going to trade shows? Are you a great speaker, comedian, networker? Or are you none of those, just a person who cares about world peace? Knowing your profile will help you hone your style.

In marketing, you need to know what is the best branding for the products and services you offer. Start by answering this question: If you could take the deepest sense or feeling that you have about your business or career, and display that sense through colors and shapes for others to see, what would your design look like?

Think of your message and brand as it might be expressed in the colors, emotions or feelings you want to evoke in your customers, infused throughout every part of your published materials from website to fliers, to business cards, to letterhead. Even the colors in your office décor can announce your brand, as it did for Sandra.

You read earlier about how Sandra left corporate America and formed her own real estate company. One of the first things she did was order all pink office supplies, an expression of her style that clients could expect: playful and smart, just goofy enough to place her services outside the corporate box she no longer fit in.

Your marketing strategy can go beyond your office décor to the shape and kind of building that holds your business and where it is located—city, suburbs, country. All can be congruent with who you are and your highest purpose to get your message out there. If your marketing strategy is aimed only at making money, then maybe a big "SALE" sign or name outside your business will be enough. But if you want to actually share your gifts and make a long-term difference in the world, and make money, the image you present needs to come from your own uniqueness and vision.

MARKETING BY PROFILE

Take a moment and think about what kind of marketing strategies you are currently using. Do they reflect your deepest purpose, the essence of who you are and what you were born to do?

Probably not—but they could be. Here are some guidelines for marketing based on the qualities of each of the profiles. When you know your own profile, you'll see how these guidelines apply uniquely, creating congruent marketing that puts your message—and personal purpose in life—out there.

The elements in your marketing and branding efforts I will describe are *color*, *theme*, *imagery*, *feel*, and *energy*. Marketing execution—the actual daily and consistent delivery of your marketing—is best done by hiring a good Knowledgeable Achiever to do it for you.

CREATIVE IDEALIST

CREATIVE IDEALISTS are incredibly ingenious and have an irreverent sense of humor. Usually they have pie-in-the-sky kinds of ideas and dreams for their business. They will attract other dreamers and people who believe in infinite possibility—if they can get their true message out there.

COLORS: Upper range of the color palette: purples, blues, magenta, and light-creating effects that seem to be expanding.

THEMES: Enlightenment, mysteries, healing, new science, spirituality, soul, higher purpose, oneness, aliens, and anything that challenges the establishment way of thinking.

IMAGERY: Angelic or spiritual images, humor of any kind (but mostly intellectual), creative art, and ways of putting together ideas through imagery to capture the imagination in ways no one else would think of. The imagery should make the viewer look up, like the ceiling paintings in the *Sagrada Familia*, Gaudí´s emblematic church in Barcelona. Other images could be hot air balloons, birds in flight, clouds, and sunsets.

FEEL: More cerebral than emotional, but breathtakingly so. The sense is not about deep feeling but rather about being taken on an exciting, fun ride.

ENERGY: High with a playful edge to it: *Up, up and away!* The energy needs to be expansive and uplifting, never down or overly serious, expressed visually with bursts of light and stars with happy faces and shiny halos.

EMOTIONAL INTELLIGENCE SPECIALIST

EMOTIONAL INTELLIGENCE SPECIALISTS are gentle, loving and soft. Their businesses are always tuned to the individual's emotional needs. They attract heart-centered people who want to be treated with gentle respect and caring.

COLORS: Pastels and soft red, orange, pink, and green to create an atmosphere of soft holding.

THEMES: Love, compassion, reverence, connection, feelings, nurturing, emotional healing, soul, and anything that melts the heart and offers a more loving connection.

IMAGERY: Any image of the heart, healing hands, flowers, children, animals and pets, Mother Mary, people embracing, angels, and anything that makes you slow down and feel.

FEEL: More emotional, not about thinking. There is a sense of going inside to what is really important in the customer's life.

ENERGY: Soft and low, never conveyed through a whole-page ad. Backgrounds may be pink with lots of space, not too much written, but some quotes from heart-centered leaders. The energy is calming and nonintrusive, letting a person feel their connection to the work or product.

TEAM PLAYER

TEAM PLAYERS are warm and embracing, making a customer feel like they are becoming part of a family and will be well taken care of. Team Player businesses are always tuned to the service needs of their clients, so they attract the people who want great service and a smile.

COLORS: Warm reds, greens, browns, orange, and rust, not colors that stand out but rather give a feeling of grounding, home, and caring.

THEMES: Service with a smile, caring, compassion, family, the client always comes first, helping hand, Good Samaritan, brotherhood, "guaranteed or your money back," and anything that makes a person feel they're being treated like family.

IMAGERY: Family pictures of the whole staff, hands shaking, hugs, Thanksgiving dinner, smiling faces, and anything that makes a person smile and trust. Team Players are simple, "salt of the earth" people, so the imagery should never be complicated.

FEEL: Being held in a warm embrace. Since this profile's business is about service, everything needs to make customers feel that there is no higher purpose in life than to make them happy.

ENERGY: Warm and friendly, loyal and dependable, and should be about the customer, not about the business person. It is strong and grounded, not too much or too little, but safe and caring. The energy of the Team Player is loving and caring, making people feel good about themselves and helping them achieve their desires through receiving great service.

CHARISMATIC LEADER-CHARMER

CHARISMATIC LEADER-CHARMERS are dynamic and inspiring, born marketers. Their businesses range from involvement with Fortune 500 companies to basement inventor, to the local psychic or healer, to running a family business. No matter what they do, they want to lead and inspire others. They attract success-driven people who want to be like them, people who need a leader to give them permission to be their own leader in their lives.

COLORS: Bold and bright, with blue and red being the primary colors; but this profile can use any color as long as it is dramatic. The colors should be vibrant, creating a sense of urgency and possibility. They are also able to use black as well to grab attention.

THEMES: Broad, including power, success, passion, fame, money, empowerment, urgency, instant healing/health/love/success. Slogans used will say such things as, "The one true pathway," "The 3 easy steps to a better…" They are also very aware that their clients' pain motivates them more than pleasure, so they use negatively charged statements aimed to trigger an emotional reaction and give little or no explanation of why their product has anything to do with that. They simply make the link and let the buyer decide how bad they want to get rid of the pain.

Since the Charismatic Leader-Charmer can express through any of the profiles, look at marketing themes for the other four profiles and then just add more energy to make it grander. For example, *Loving Energy Healing* for the Emotional Intelligence Specialist becomes *Ascended Master Attunement*. *Join our Family* for the Team Player becomes *Become Part of Our Worldwide Movement*. Charismatic Leader-Charmer marketing includes anything that motivates people to do more in their lives and feel empowered, like Nike's *Just Do It!*, *Find Your Greatness*, and *Winning Takes Care of Everything*, and Apple's *Think Different*, *The Power to Be Your Best*, and *PC vs. Mac*.

IMAGERY: Takes advantage of the power of iconic symbols. Most of the powerful marketing in the world is created by Charismatic Leader-Charmers who get to the top and know that staying there is a matter of keeping themselves in the minds of the people in a specific way. Nike uses world-class athletes and imagery of people who are winners or are in the act of being great. Apple aims their message to the intellectual and creative achievers by using pictures of people who have changed the world with a thought or song.

FEEL: Emotional, dramatic. The more Charismatic Leader-Charmers can evoke drama and emotion, good or bad, the closer they are to selling people their version of success. When people see their marketing, they should feel the message more than think it.

ENERGY: Bigger than life, cutting edge. Charismatic Leader-Charmers take out the multi-page ads and are great on video or radio because of their inspirational message. Their energy motivates people to feel their passion and take a chance to be the success they have always desired themselves to be.

KNOWLEDGEABLE ACHIEVER

KNOWLEDGEABLE ACHIEVERS are a combination of both form and function. They give people the tools and strategies to be more efficient and achieve success through buying the smartest product or equipment to get the job done. They run large or small companies and businesses focused on helping people be more successful by using intelligence, and well-researched and proven systems. They are not born marketers but will sell by comparing their product to inferior products to show they have the highest quality. They attract people who want the best and want to know a step-by-step system to be more successful in their business, get a date, be a better parent, win a triathlon, have better health, or whatever it is they desire to achieve.

KNOWLEDGEABLE ACHIEVER

COLORS: Solids—but not a lot of them. Preferring not to appeal to emotions, they do best with black, white and grey in graphic ads or with a white background in videos.

THEMES: Always to the point and direct. Knowledgeable Achievers think in black and white: *This is good, buy it*, or *This is bad, don't buy it*. Themes will appeal to an educated buyer: *Do this and get that in the shortest time possible with the best results*. They tend to pick businesses that already have a high demand, and then set about creating the image in people's heads that they are better than the competition. The big screen TV companies sell more by statistics than what can actually be seen. If it is a service, the theme will be how they have the best and most efficient offering, appealing with slogans like, *Try all the others first, then come see us*. Natural systems people, Knowledgeable Achievers do well with the theme of teaching steps needed to succeed in any activity.

IMAGERY: Actual pictures or art work presented clearly and simply. These are the more corporate kinds of images that use basic geometrical shapes aimed not to confuse clients but build confidence in product or service. Graphics should directly depict the product in some way; for example, advertising for a speaking coach that depicts a person speaking, for an appliance store a refrigerator, for a pharmacy a pill, and for an auto mechanic business a car with hood open. The use of symbols shouldn't be abstract or emotional, but rather clarify what the product is and what the buyer will get.

FEEL: It's never about feelings or emotion but rather about education and quality. The Knowledgeable Achiever knows that if customers know what a product can do for them, is given verifiable statistics of the full value, and the price is below that value, they will get the sale. Feeling is a smaller part of the sale for this profile than for the Charismatic Leader-Charmer, Emotional Intelligence Specialist, or Team Player.

> ENERGY: That of getting the job done on time and effortlessly. There is a sense of mastery, like that of a concert violinist who strikes a balance between effort and preciseness. A sense of confidence, strength, and discipline is reflected in every area of the Knowledgeable Achiever's business and marketing. These energetic qualities inspire us all to study harder, work for our goals more efficiently, and be a success internally through personal achievement, and externally through strategy and wisdom.

Knowing your profile—or better yet, the combination of your top two profiles—helps you make sure that the message of the business you are sharing in the world actually awakens others the way you want it to, while at the same time attracts your perfect customers.

Of course, we can all take lessons on marketing from the Charismatic Leader-Charmers, who are the best at getting attention and convincing people to buy their products. But be careful not to try to be a Charismatic Leader-Charmer in your marketing strategy if you don't have that profile. The key to good marketing and being able to inspire the world is to be congruent in yourself first, aligning all your actions and choices with your own life purpose. Then, when your purpose is congruent with the message you deliver to your customers and the world through *colors*, *themes*, *imagery*, *feeling*, and *energy*, you can't help but have extraordinary success in your marketing and business.

NEXT ...

At Level 3, I'll teach you how to hire and manage a team of people who are not just showing up each day for work, but who love to come to work because each one is in a job that fulfills their purpose in life. In the next chapter, you'll learn how to use the Profile System to hire staff in a way that fills individual needs and creates a culture of wholeness.

LEVEL THREE

CREATE A PURPOSE CENTERED *Culture* at work

Chapter Eight
HIRE ON PURPOSE WITH THE PROFILES

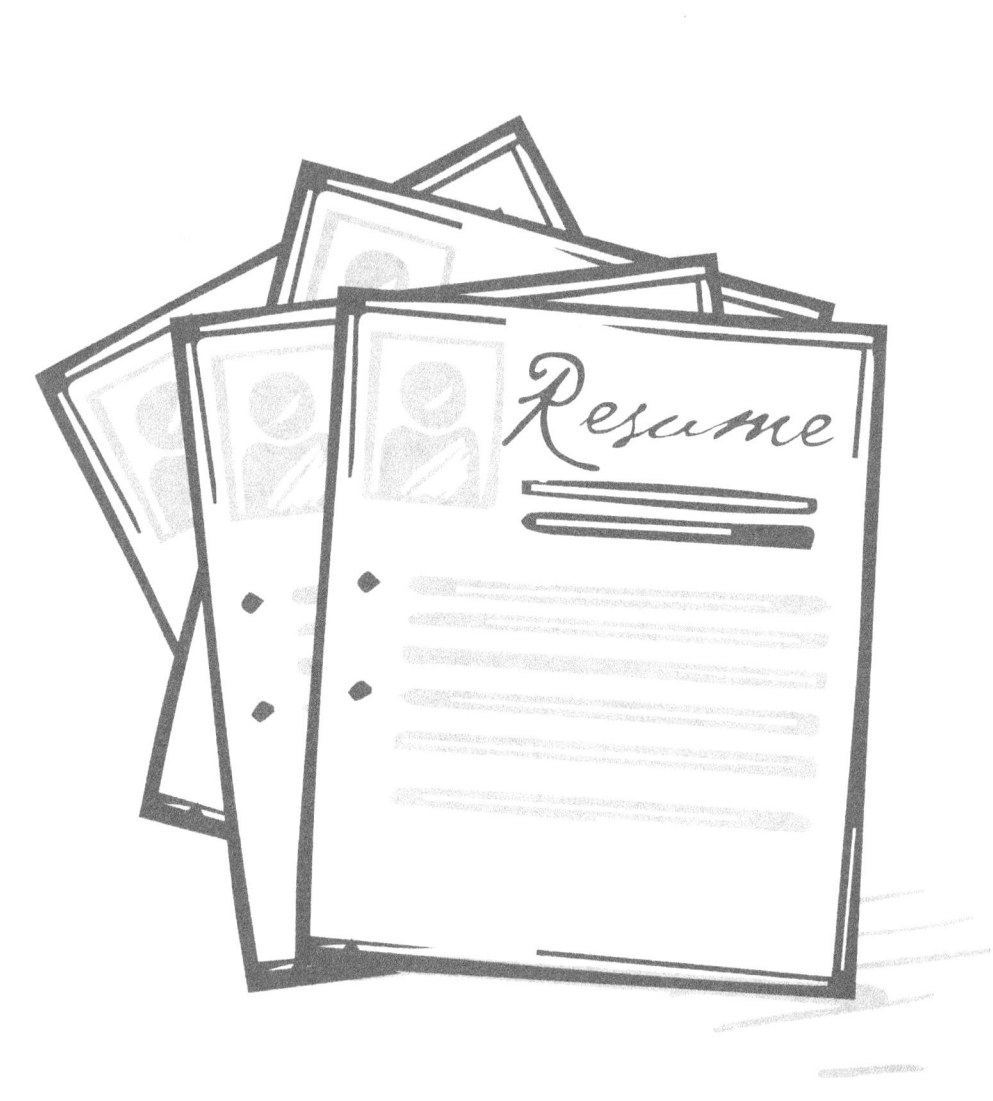

CHAPTER 8
HIRE ON PURPOSE WITH THE PROFILES

As a business owner or manager hiring a staff, you want to fill positions with people best suited for the job who will stay in the job. High turnover rates hurt your company and hurt your bottom line, as well as increase your stress level and that of your employees, so it's important you make the best hire possible.

A strong resume is often what convinces management to hire. However, a person's past experience may not reflect what they are innately designed to do, and so resumes alone can be misleading. Follow best hiring practices and take your time: do your homework, interview, check every reference, (ask for more, especially if they have changed jobs frequently, as might a Charismatic Leader-Charmer), and give a prospective hire a trial week/month before bringing them more permanently on board.

Determining a person's profile so you can match profile to position can further ensure that your hiring efforts are successful. The Profile System can help you decide who to hire to fill that accounting position, or balance out your marketing team, or put on the floor in sales or customer service. Jobs, like people, have energetic qualities, and when people and their work are matched according to their profile qualities, it's a win-win for everyone.

In this chapter, we'll take a look at key positions and see how they are best filled by people in each of the five profiles to create a successful, purpose-centered business.

HIRE THE PROFILE, NOT THE EXPERIENCE

So how do you assess the profile of someone you are considering hiring? In

Level 1 and 2 of this book, you've read about the core qualities and defenses demonstrated in each of the five profiles, making it possible for you to have a good idea of a potential hire's primary and secondary profile. Further, I've provided a chart in the Appendix of this book for you to quickly read anyone's profile based on their physical and energetic appearance. Then, in an interview, you can ask questions to draw out the person's deeper truth. Once you are in the final stages of interviewing, you can have the person take the online *Business Profile Self-Assessment* available on my website.

As the Profile System is designed, we all have a combination of the five profile qualities in our makeup. To some degree, each person has the ability to be creative, to be compassionate, to be supportive, and to have leadership and organizational skills. But for each person, one of those qualities will stand out in how they will excel when given the opportunity in the right job.

Great managers and human resource people innately know that there is a special quality in a person that fits the job they seek to fill. Because of this, they hire for character and then train that person for skill. They know if you hire the wrong character for the job, even with the greatest skills and background, the person will have difficulty succeeding and you will not be happy with that employee.

MATCH THE POSITION TO THE PROFILE

Depending on the job you need to fill, some profiles will be a better fit than others. For example, to fill a sales position, you need a person who has a strong, internal *I want to win* drive and who also has some charm. You want them to have enough people-skills to know what the customer is going to need in order to buy what they really want. A good sales person finds a way to make the customer pay the highest price for the product because it means a higher commission for them.

Yup, you guessed it. A Charismatic Leader-Charmer is good in a sales position. If you put a Team Player or Emotional Intelligence Specialist in a sales position, that person is not going to get to the bottom line in the same way as a Charismatic Leader-Charmer. A Team Player or Emotional

Intelligence Specialist will focus on giving the customer what they need without caring much about making money. They'll always take less if it makes the customer happy, even at times when a deal amounts to giving away the farm. Charismatic Leader-Charmers, on the other hand, realize when a customer wants something and can afford it and so will push for a more profitable sale, always mindful that both they and the company need a profit to stay afloat.

Overlapping qualities as they appear within the profiles can be confusing at first. When hiring a Director or COO, you might choose a Charismatic Leader-Charmer, but you could be asking for trouble, because Charismatic Leader-Charmers can sometimes behave chaotically. A good director needs to know how to schedule and organize the business' activities and be able to understand all areas—a job better suited to the Knowledgeable Achiever. As leaders, Charismatic Leader-Charmers are better suited for positions such as founder or CEO, where they can bring vision as well as passion and volatility with little or no consequence.

A Knowledgeable Achiever in the position of director would know the profiles of all the staff and how people should best be assigned roles within the organization. They might put a Team Player in customer service, a job that is not expected to make a lot of money for the company and so fits the Team Player profile, paying them at the level where they're comfortable and for their value to the business.

Charismatic Leader-Charmers and Knowledgeable Achievers make the most money for companies and will demand higher salaries for their positions. Team Players or Emotional Intelligence Specialists will thrive by connecting with people and do not generate revenue like the Charismatic Leader-Charmers and Knowledgeable Achievers do, and so will be at a lower pay grade and be happy at that level.

AVOID THESE HIRING MISTAKES

I came into business from a background as an athlete, a tennis professional, so my business training was minimal. But I was driven, and at age 23 I ran a country club with 15 pros working under me. I made all the mistakes in hiring and in managing people a typical business owner makes, including hiring people who looked great on paper and appeared to be go-getters like me. But I soon found out these people couldn't maintain their focus and didn't care about making my business succeed—because while they had fit my standards and appeared good on paper, they were in the wrong job for them!

After creating the Life Purpose Profiles, I was able to apply it to my business immediately in the area of hiring. First in my tennis business with a dozen employees, then in my school with over 30 staff members. I realized after hiring the perfect people for jobs that one of the biggest mistakes employers make is in trying to hire themselves—people who think like they do and work like they do.

When you've hired people like yourself, you'll need to defend your position from those who try to undermine you to get your job or they have nothing new to offer. When you hire people with different sets of skills than yours, they complement your strengths and thus do things you don't want to do, freeing you to do what is your strength.

Another mistake business owners make, especially if it's a highly competitive business, is to hire all Knowledgeable Achievers and Charismatic Leader-Charmers—the go-getters and movers and shakers. But then, when customers who have the other three profiles want to do business with you, they can't relate to anyone on your staff. The result is a lack of balance, and a team that is lopsided and insufficient to serve the widest range of customers.

MATCHING POSITIONS TO INDIVIDUAL NEEDS

Each of the five profiles has a different need to be fulfilled by their role in your business. When you as a manager hire staff in positions that fit their unique needs, you will have a happy team working for you, one that is successful in serving your clients and customers.

As you become more familiar with the profile qualities, you understand that creative people need to have something new and exciting going on

(Creative Idealists); feeling people need to have a deep connection with others (Emotional Intelligence Specialists); supportive people need to be in a group (Team Players); achievers need to see ever-expanding opportunities for accomplishment (Knowledgeable Achievers); and leaders need to be serving as CEOs and founders, the movers-and-shakers in any organization (Charismatic Leaders-Charmers).

When you conside hiring someone, you want to make sure the job they're being considered for supports the deeper need that is uniquely theirs—the creative need, the feeling need, the companionship need, the achievement need, or the leadership need. If you can't match person to job, no one will be happy, and the only way for anyone to succeed will be to fake it.

As a manager, you'll find that two of the most common people you want to hire are the Charismatic Leader-Charmer and the Team Player. Both will give superior service to customers, but it's important to be aware that there's a broad difference between these two types of people and how they operate. For example, you might hire a Team Player—those warm, friendly people who do anything you ask them to do—for a sales job. They can offer great customer service, but they can't close the deal in a way that is beneficial to the business because they don't distinguish between the value of the product and the benefit to the customer.

The Charismatic Leader-Charmer, however, naturally knows how to connect to people but also how to be clear that, bottom line, the sale needs to make a profit. Unlike the Team Player, the Charismatic Leader-Charmer will do whatever it takes to make sure the customer knows it's the best thing they've ever done to buy your product.

In a reverse situation, if you are hiring for a team position, don't ever put the Charismatic Leader-Charmer in an environment where people have to get along and help each other out because the Charismatic Leader-Charmer won't thrive. Unlike the Team Player, the Charismatic Leader-Charmer tends to be highly competitive and wants to get individual credit for a win. They are wired to stand out and be special, while Team Players are the ones who do most of the work and then proudly say, *It was a team effort.*

BUILDING A STRONG TEAM

A great business creates a culture in which everyone is deeply aligned with their job description. Because they are in the right jobs for them, staff all work together to support each other for a common goal: the success of the business. Each person is valued equally because each person has a unique role that is suited to their most innate qualities.

Conversely, top-down, hierarchical structures don't value human uniqueness, but rather see people as having degrees of value depending on what they contribute to the business. But when there is balance and unity in your staff, your business works as a whole, all parts in the perfect place and functioning smoothly to move forward more effectively.

Business leaders who understand this put themselves in with their staff and enjoy being on the same level, rather than setting up a corporate hierarchy where as top dog they must protect their position from aspiring staff. You hire people very differently when you're not trying to protect your position; instead your goal is to surround yourself with strong people whose deeper purpose can be fulfilled in their role. The result is less stress and more productivity.

Acknowledging strengths is a better way to manage than simply filling positions with people doing the things you don't want to do in your business. The message you want to convey is: *I'm giving you this job because you will be so much better than I am at this.* A humble leader is always the leader who is the most powerful.

ATTRACTING THE BEST CUSTOMERS AND CLIENTS

Understanding how each profile attracts the perfect customers and clients for them helps you to place people in jobs where they will be the most productive, most happy, and most likely to be successful at what they do.

CREATIVE IDEALIST

THE CREATIVE IDEALIST will attract people who are looking for a new way to do something, maybe even seeking a mystical kind of connection. People who are ready to change up will be attracted to the Creative Idealist.

EMOTIONAL INTELLIGENCE SPECIALIST

THE EMOTIONAL INTELLIGENCE SPECIALIST will attract customers who need to be taken step by step and not pushed, but prefer a soft approach. If you've got a business where people need a one-on-one talk, you'll want a person who is emotionally fit to deal with them.

TEAM PLAYER

A TEAM PLAYER placed in customer service is going to be working with people who need help. Their supportive, caring qualities naturally attract and work best with people who need a lot of help.

CHARISMATIC LEADER-CHARMER

The Charismatic Leader-Charmer is going to attract people who want to be inspired and will buy a product simply because the person on stage is so motivating.

THE KNOWLEDGEABLE ACHIEVER

THE KNOWLEDGEABLE ACHIEVER attracts people who want to be shown a structured system for how to get from A to B. Only the Knowledgeable Achiever can deliver that kind of service to those who come to your business for the shortest line between here and there.

THE PROFILES WORK AT EVERY LEVEL

When you use the Profile System to hire, you not only hire the best people for jobs, you also have a tool to teach those you hire how to best deliver their unique gifts to customers or clients. Then, staff can learn to read the profiles of their customers or clients and deliver to them what it is they want, as you did for them.

And so it goes down the ladder: You pick your staff, giving them the roles they need to be fulfilled and happy. Then your staff gets trained in the Profile System, so they know who their customers are and how to best serve them. This is how the Profile System can work at every level.

In my own business, an energy medicine training school, I work with a staff of 30 people that facilitate over 100 students on the training weekends of my three-year program. My main teachers are in charge of 20 students and they must be either Knowledgeable Achievers or Charismatic Leader-Charmers, or a combination of both, because as a main teacher the person needs to have a big presence to be able to take charge of a large group and also keep a tight, safe container for the deep work we do.

Each main teacher in a class has a five-person support team composed of one of each of the profiles. My strategy is to have a leader in each class, and for support, a Team Player, an Emotional Intelligence Specialist, a Creative Idealist, and then either a Charismatic Leader-Charmer or Knowledgeable Achiever, depending on the leader's profile. This assures that inside every room there is a person on my staff that everyone in that room can relate to.

Covering all the profiles is an important element of what I do in my business. The benefit is I get feedback from each one about particular situations that happen in class. When I talk to each of the staff, I'll get a completely different view of what happened, based on how they experienced it from their view. In this way, I learn more about what is actually happening in my business than I could ever get by relying only on my own view of it.

When I hire support people for other areas of my business, I always hire Knowledgeable Achievers and Team Players, and hopefully people who are a combination of the two, primary and secondary. My graphics and technical people are often Knowledgeable Achievers with a secondary profile as Team

Players, meaning they are organized enough to do the job and also care about me and want my business to succeed. They have to have a Team Player quality because I need them to care more about my business than I do, since as a Creative Idealist my strength is in creating new ideas and not in sticking to a schedule. If instead they have a strong Charismatic Leader-Charmer in their profile, they are likely to take on big jobs but not necessarily care about my business succeeding. They are more interested in becoming the best graphic designer than in supporting my aims.

Having the kind of support I need around me, allows me to just be me. I'm never in a position where I don't have to be my Creative Idealist. I can try on all the other hats, but the truth is, everyone needs me to be who I am, because that's what they signed on for. They want me to be who I am, so they can be who they are. And when everyone is being who they truly are, it all works!

MAUREEN'S STORY: MANAGING STAFF WITH COMPASSION AND HUMANITY

Maureen Maloney was a graphic designer for over 30 years and for much of her career she was self-employed. But a divorce and a new partner put her on the path of asking what was her Big Why.

When she met him, the man who became her new partner owned a small dairy and did home deliveries, just like the milkman from long ago. Knowing Maureen was a foodie, he asked her to develop a granola product to sell alongside of the milk. She started playing around with different recipes, still keeping one foot in her graphic design business. Then she took the leap to rent space in a small bakery and hired a staff. The courage for making this change came from a new understanding of herself that was revealed during the three-year course she took at the Rhys Thomas Institute.

"I'd been doing self-study programs for 10 years, but when I got to Rhys' school, I was able to connect the dots of everything I'd done before," Maureen said. "I discovered I'd buried the courageous leader part of myself, my Charismatic Leader-Charmer, and was hiding behind an Emotional Intelligence Specialist/Poor Me with a heavy dose of people-pleasing of the Team Player."

Her new self-understanding not only allowed her to start a new business, it led to her hiring people that were sent from an occupational rehab program and were deemed "hard to place." Her management style as a Charismatic Leader-Charmer enabled her to work with these people—a staff of six. Here's what she said about that experience:

"My employees continue to tell me stories that attest to my leadership abilities based on my humanity, compassion, and empathy, and also about me being able to make it fun and produce an incredible product. They love to work for me."

In hiring her staff, she made sure all five profiles were represented, and found she treated people with more compassion when she knows their profile, especially someone like a Poor Me (Emotional Intelligence Specialist): "In the past, I had zero tolerance for people playing the victim card. I'm the youngest of seven, from an Irish Catholic family, so don't be crying on my shoulder!"

But now her attitude has shifted. "I've learned every profile has a beautiful gift, and I want to focus on the core instead of dealing with ugly defenses that might pop up. Knowing my employees' profiles has helped me to look at their star qualities—and the shadow side, too, giving me greater compassion."

In her first year, Maureen's company grossed six figures. She started small with local distribution, but now she's taking another leap and going for national distribution.

"Everything I've done in my life to this point has helped me to be a leader in my business. It just took knowing who I am to give me the courage to do it."

Chapter Nine
Manage & Motivate Your Staff for Great Performance

CHAPTER 9
MANAGE AND MOTIVATE YOUR STAFF FOR GREAT PERFORMANCE

As you have seen in earlier chapters, each of the profiles has an innate pull toward certain gifts and deliverables. These are not learned behaviors, but rather emerge effortlessly and are innate. Whether they are a *creative person*, a *feeler*, a *supporter*, a *leader*, or an *achiever*, that same quality can become diverted into a negative response due to workplace challenges.

Managing your staff for optimal performance involves knowing the core qualities of staff members as well as the defensive qualities that each of them embodies in their individual profile. Each becomes defensive consistently and predictably within their profile group (see chart below) with reactive behaviors that come out under stress. Creative people get lost in overthinking, feelers are easily overwhelmed, supporters can't say no, leaders dominate and manipulate, and achievers become rigid and inflexible.

These are the self-sabotaging patterns that cause untold problems when not managed at work.

PROFILE QUALITIES IN CORE AND DEFENSE

CREATIVE IDEALIST
(creative/playful)—Thinker (head spinning/dissociated/avoidant)

EMOTIONAL INTELLIGENCE SPECIALIST
(loving/reverent)—Poor Me (hypersensitive/overwhelmed)

TEAM PLAYER
(best friend/helpful/sacrificing)—People Pleaser (servant/resentful/can't say no)

> **CHARISMATIC LEADER-CHARMER**
> (inspiring/attractive)—Enforcer-Seducer (dominating/manipulative/controlling)

KNOWLEDGEABLE ACHIEVER
(wisdom/mastery/organized)—Rule Keeper (rigid/ critical/workaholic)

In this chapter, I contrast two hypothetical scenarios: first, what it looks like when staff members deal with a stressful workplace situation from their profile defense; and second, how staff can work well when each of the members knows their real value and gifts. Following that, I'll show you some basic techniques for getting your staff out of defense and back into their most resourceful state, so they can be productive and support each other for great team performance.

The work environment is a place where people feel pressure to be someone they are not—especially if they have been placed in the wrong jobs for their type—and so people often spend much of their energy in defense patterns of behavior and thought. When in defense, it seems that in order to be successful, they need to be better, smarter, stronger, and more aggressive than they naturally are. The irony is that if people just trusted their instincts and were willing to express their own flavor of power, they would have more energy, joy, and success in the work they do.

In the following workplace scenario, you will see how each of the five kinds of people respond to a stressful event, creating a chaotic situation where things just get worse, not better.

SCENARIO #1 — STAFF IN DEFENSE

> At the small company We Manage You Corp., a five-member team is approaching a deadline for a major project that will make or break the company. Their client is Persnickety International, Inc., an import/export business. If the team produces the product on time as promised, all employees have been told they'll get large, end-of-year bonuses. If they don't, Persnickety International gets the job for 25 percent less in cost, and in that case half the team will likely be laid off.

The project is three-quarters of the way done and has used more manpower than was originally estimated, forcing everyone to work overtime. Stress levels are high but get even higher when five days before the deadline, the president of Persnickety International, Mr. Deal Breaker, pays an unexpected visit to the company's offices. Barging in on the workday, he announces that things have changed in his business and tells the entire team that he needs the product in two days, not five. And with a little grin he says, "If it isn't done by then, the deal is off—I won't honor the contract."

The room is quiet after Mr. Deal Breaker makes his announcement. Then people start to react, each one coming from the defensive side of their individual profile.

Tim the Thinker, standing in the back of the room as he likes to do much of the time, fidgets nervously. His mind is spinning with a million ways to handle the stressful situation, but he's afraid to do or say any of them and risk confrontation of any kind. He's likely to not even hear the grumblings of the other employees as he heads for his cubicle. His defense is spinning in his head and avoiding conflict.

Portia the Poor Me, sitting down near the water cooler, is feeling exhausted from the stress. She turns to her co-worker and begins complaining about how awful it will be if she has to work one more extra shift, and how depressed she already is that the deal might fall through. She says nothing to Mr. Deal Breaker, just looks sadly at him, and uses the situation to whine, feel victimized, and get the other staff members emotionally upset. She may even call in sick the next day. She says, "I can't help how I feel, Mr. Deal Breaker is so mean and unreasonable! Does he think we are machines that can work 24/7?" Portia's defense is to get overwhelmed easily, complain, then collapse.

Peter the People Pleaser, sitting in the middle of the room with the bulk of the project's work on his desk, is the next person to react. He approaches Mr. Deal Breaker and assumes that if the client needs the job done early, there must be a really good reason, and so with a "we can solve anything" smile, he asks if there is anything he can do to help. Mr. Deal Breaker gives him the keys to his car with instructions to get a briefcase containing a list of changes to the deal. When Peter returns, Mr. Deal Breaker pulls out a thick folder with all the changes he wants done and says with no word of thanks, "Here you go, figure out the changes in two days or no deal," and walks away.

Peter turns three shades of red but bites back on his anger because he'd never say anything to reflect badly on the company but silently resents that he's been so nice to such a jerk. Peter's defense is to be overly self-sacrificing and then feel burdened, unable to ask for help or set a boundary.

At this point, office manager **Rhonda the Rule Keeper,** who handles the contracts, sees what is going on and invites Mr. Deal Breaker to step into her office to discuss his issue. After hearing him out, she tells him that the signed contract between We Manage You Corp and Persnickety International is legal and binding, and what he is trying to do is inappropriate and unnecessary. The team will have the project done on time as the contract states, and if he breaks the contract, he will hear from the company law firm. She reminds him that the contract terms state that all legal fees are to be paid by him if there needs to be litigation.

Mr. Deal Breaker reacts strongly, saying he doesn't care about the original deal. He asserts that We Manage You Corp stands to make millions from him over the next few years, and if they don't play ball with him, he'll take his business elsewhere. Rhonda the Rule Keeper assures him that changing at this late date would be impossible. We Manage You Corp. will only honor the contract as written. Rhonda gets up and shows Mr. Deal Breaker to the door, dismissing him abruptly and closing the door firmly behind him. Her defense is to be inflexible and strictly obedient to the letter of the law with no room for any kind of compromise or negotiation.

Mr. Deal Breaker heads toward the elevator, muttering angrily under his breath that he will never do business with this "crappy" company again.

Finally, **Ernest the Enforcer-Seducer**, president of the company who was playing golf that morning and missed the fireworks, gets the abbreviated version from his secretary and heads Mr. Deal Breaker off at the elevator. He approaches Mr. Deal Breaker aggressively, getting six inches from his face, and says loudly, "You're not going anywhere!" He walks the client back into his office and with a snarl tells his secretary to hold all his calls.

Once inside the office, the president engages Mr. Deal Breaker without letting him sit down. Glaring into his eyes he growls, "I hear you're trying to break our deal. Who the #*&^%!! do you think you are?" Mr. Deal Breaker doesn't back down, but responds that he doesn't care what the deal was, he wants a new deal or else.

Raising his voice so everyone in the building can hear him, Ernest the Enforcer says, "No one screws me or my company. The deal stands!"

Mr. Deal Breaker gets up, says he has never been treated so rudely, and heads for the door. But Ernest gets there first and pins himself between Mr. Deal Breaker and the door. Then, three inches from Mr. Deal Breaker's ear, he says in a barely audible tone, "You know, I've got a friend in customs, and one phone call by me could bring your import/export business to a grinding halt. All it takes is my friend finding something that's not supposed to be in one of your import containers." Ernest's defense is to get his way through force and threats, pulling out all the punches to make someone bend to his will.

Mr. Deal Breaker recoils at the threat and exclaims, "You wouldn't dare…!"

"You keep to our deal or I call my friend…." Ernest the Enforcer says. Having met his match, Mr. Deal Breaker skulks out of the office but is determined to not give up. As he takes the elevator down, his thoughts are filled with visions of revenge and he fumbles with his phone to dial his lawyer.

You have just seen the five most common reactive patterns people exhibit in the workplace when dealing with a stressful situation: avoidance, overwhelm, resentment, inflexibility, and aggression. In the next scenario, you'll see how people who know their profiles, and also the profiles of others they are dealing with, respond to the same stressful events. But this time, instead of spiraling into chaos, they are able head off a disaster for a more positive outcome.

SCENARIO #2 — TEAMWORK THAT WINS

Mr. Deal Breaker arrives at the offices of We Manage You Corp. and makes his pronouncement. The room is quiet. The first to react is **Peter the Team Player** (formerly the *People Pleaser*). Peter heads straight for the office manager's office to set up a team meeting to immediately deal with the crisis.

Portia the Emotional Intelligence Specialist (formerly the *Poor Me*) approaches Mr. Deal Breaker, who she senses is under enormous stress himself, and makes friendly eye contact. She assures him in empathic tones that he has been heard and is going to be able to get his needs met. She quietly tells him that the team will all want to hear what his needs are, and it will take a few minutes get the team together. Then she asks about his family and lets the conversation move to his day and how he feels about the pressure this deal has put on him.

Peter the Team Player comes out of the office with the office manager, **Rhonda the Knowledgeable Achiever** (formerly the *Rule Keeper*). She politely asks Mr. Deal Breaker to join the entire creative team in the conference room where the new proposal can be communicated and dealt with.

Peter the Team Player asks if he can get Mr. Deal Breaker some coffee or anything else that he might need. When he hears that Mr. Deal Breaker has left important papers in his car, Peter jumps at the opportunity to retrieve them and delegates the coffee, water and cookies to another staff member.

As everyone is entering the conference room, Rhonda calls the president of We Manage You Corp., **Charismatic Leader-Charmer Ernest** (formerly the *Enforcer-Seducer*) and after informing him of the situation, asks him to join the meeting a half-hour into it.

Once in the conference room, Rhonda runs the meeting, and other staff members swing into action: Team Player Peter makes sure that Mr. Deal Breaker has everything he needs and is attended to; Emotional Intelligence Specialist Portia positions herself next to Mr. Deal Breaker to help tone down any volatility, and **Creative Idealist Tim** (formerly the *Thinker*) gets the computer and audio-video equipment ready for the group to explore any and all new possibilities.

The opening discussion centers around Mr. Deal Breaker's leadership in his industry and the contributions his company has made toward making the world a better place. Mr. Deal Breaker beams positively with the acknowledgement and starts to relax in his urgency about the project getting done sooner than planned.

Knowledgeable Achiever Rhonda further acknowledges Mr. Deal Breaker's Charismatic Leader-Charmer quality by informing him that We Manage You Corp. is honored to work on this project and reassures him that the resources of the company are fully at his disposal. She then asks Mr. Deal Breaker to outline his needs and vision for the project and what has changed that he feels he must have delivery earlier than agreed.

Mr. Deal Breaker is now feeling supported by a group he assumed would be on the defensive. He carefully explains his predicament:

"I'm sorry to bring you this news, but my timetable has moved up due an overseas issue," he begins. "I need the product in two days if it's to ship to Japan before an increased tariff goes into effect that would make the deal a financial loss. If I can't get the product shipped in two days, I'm going to have to cancel the order. Sadly, if I don't have what I need in two days, the deal's off."

Rhonda the Knowledgeable Achiever clearly sees the big picture here. She asks Creative Idealist Tim to project the timeline and contingency issues on an overhead, and asks him for his suggestions. Tim comes up with three options to get the job done in two days and displays them for all to see: 1) Do a product redesign that is untested but eliminates one step in the process, 2) scrub the finished package done in the last three days and have the packaging shipped later for overseas assembly, or 3) increase manpower on the project to get it done sooner with a 30 percent increase in cost.

Knowledgeable Achiever Rhonda dismisses the first two options because they might reflect badly on both the company and the seller, and chooses the third option to up manpower hours. She turns to Team Player Peter for his opinion on what is possible, manpower-wise. Peter replies there is no time to bring new team members up to speed, but if the existing team worked 12-hour shift rotations, they could likely get it done in three days; two days is impossible.

The president of the company, Charismatic Leader-Charmer Ernest, shows up and gets briefed on the team's findings. First, he compliments his staff for the fantastic job they have done. Then he lets Mr. Deal Breaker know he understands fully about the tariff changes and has been doing his own digging for a solution. He asks if he can meet with Mr. Deal Breaker in private before the meeting proceeds further.

The two go off into an adjoining office, and the president addresses his client:

"If I can solve your problem of getting the product into Japan without the new tariff, do we have our deal?" He pauses respectfully and then continues. "We don't want to lose you as a loyal customer, and I know you don't want to lose the millions that this deal represents for you."

Ernest then reveals that he has a friend in customs who has an internal form that can be filled out for companies needing a slight extension, totally legal, but also at the discretion of the agent who owes him a favor. This can ensure that the product will get to its destination without the normal waiting period. Mr. Deal Breaker responds that he'll accept the offer if it can be guaranteed.

Ernest says, "I want to be totally above board on this. I can make the paperwork happen, we can increase the work hours and accelerate production to get it all done in three days, which will get you what you want and not kill my amazing staff." He paused and then continued. "Making this change will increase production costs by 30 percent since I'll have to pay time and a half to the staff when they work the extra hours, and give them time off once the project is done. As a valued customer, I'll only increase the bottom line 20 percent and absorb the other 10. I feel this is the absolute best we can do and that it's a win-win." Mr. Deal Breaker nods in assent.

The two men return to the conference room to join the group. Ernest addresses the group, announcing that the team will need to have the product out the door in three days, not two, which is only possible if everyone works double shifts until it is done. As a motivation, he tells them they will all get time-and-a-half as well as a four-day paid weekend, since the project ends two days ahead of schedule. All agree, and Mr. Deal Breaker is satisfied with the outcome.

It's likely that Persnickety International will do a lot more business with We Manage You Corp. in the future—without the need for legal counsel or action!

As you can see, there are many options available to manage a breakdown in the workplace for people who know their own and others' profiles, and few options when people are reacting from their defenses.

The Profile System helps staff and management understand and avoid defensive behaviors that block authentic and positive reactions in the moment, and lead to bigger problems down the line. The result is a smoother, less stressful workplace environment, one that doesn't risk business and financial losses from people reacting defensively.

Supporting Creative Idealists to share their new ideas, Emotional Intelligence Specialists to help people calm down, Team Players to give their brand of great service, Knowledgeable Achievers to make the plan run gracefully, and Charismatic Leader-Charmers to motivate and inspire, will nip self-sabotaging patterns in the bud before they can destroy client confidence and send your business into chaos.

STRATEGIES TO MOTIVATE STAFF

As a manager or leader, when any member of your staff becomes stuck and is not being productive, you can manage and motivate them so they deliver their greatest gifts, not their shadow defenses. Even within a team, when people know their co-workers' profile strengths and weaknesses, they can act together to support and motivate each other in specific ways.

The motivation for someone to get out of a negative, self-sabotaging pattern is different for each one of the five profiles. Knowing how they sabotage themselves helps you to know what to do—*and not do*—to help them return to a productive state where they can get what they really want, not what their profile shadow gets them.

Think of your staff members who might fit each profile described below in defense. You can powerfully motivate them when you utilize the following strategies:

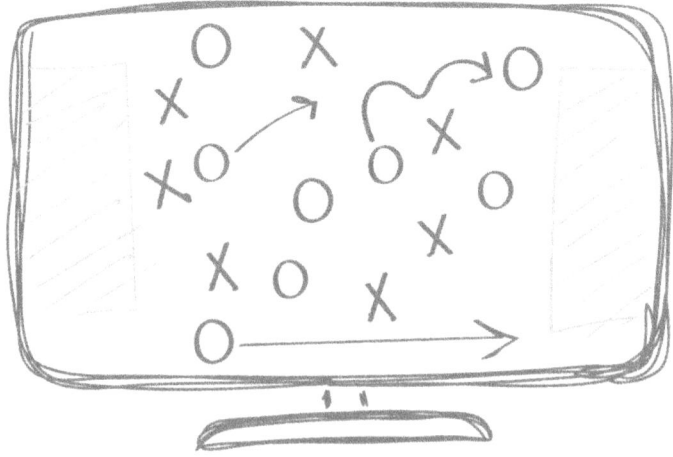

THE THINKER (CREATIVE IDEALIST)

Thinkers maintain high levels of fear and anxiety that keep them mentally spinning and unable to make clear decisions. As a result, their brilliance and creativity rarely materialize into products or services that make a difference.

Their inner dialogue is: ***Other people don't value my ideas and will reject me for them.***

When supporting the Thinker to return to their Creative Idealist:

1. Never tell them to quit goofing off and get organized; let them be all over the place in their expression without judgment or censure.
2. Value their ideas first, no matter how crazy sounding, and then ask questions.
3. Accept that what appears to be distracted attention is actually a creative level of presence.
4. Never be aggressive with them physically or emotionally.

THE POOR ME (EMOTIONAL INTELLIGENCE SPECIALIST)

Poor Me's are easily overwhelmed by conflict or stress, allowing the words or actions of others to deeply hurt them. Once deeply hurt, they become helpless and incapacitated to the point of giving up.

Their inner dialogue is: ***Other people don't care enough, because I am not enough.***

When supporting the Poor Me's to return to their Emotional Intelligence Specialist:

1. Acknowledge the value of their feelings.
2. Never tell them to toughen up and get over their feelings or that they are being too emotional.
3. Let them know you see how compassionate they are and how much heart they put into everything they do.
4. Remind them that their sensitivity is their greatest strength, making them courageous not weak.

THE PEOPLE PLEASER (TEAM PLAYER)

People Pleasers get stuck in never being able to saying no and then becoming resentful of being taken advantage of. They get grumpy when they think they're doing all the work and no one else is helping as much. They will stay in abusive relationships where they are responsible for what goes on 80 per cent of the time and their partners only 20 percent.

Their inner dialogue is: ***Other people don't appreciate me.***

When supporting the People Pleaser to return to their Team Player:

1. Don't require them to think independently and resolve conflicts on their own; instead, give them suggestions for what to do.
2. Assure them that you appreciate and value them for the services they perform. Be specific and give details.
3. Never advise them to just "go it alone" and start their own business; they always need to work with partners.
4. Recognize that they can't say no and go against someone else in need, and remind them that their no's are often yes's to themselves.

THE ENFORCER-SEDUCER (CHARISMATIC LEADER-CHARMER)

Enforcer-Seducers never trust anyone out of fear of betrayal. They self-sabotage through aggression or battling for control, or through defensive behaviors of any of the other pro-files, especially the Poor Me.

Their inner dialogue is: *You can't trust anyone, keep everyone under control.*

When supporting the Enforcer-Seducer to return to their Charismatic Leader-Charmer:

1. Remind them that as a leader, they must decide what they are for and not what they are against.

2. Encourage them to get out and talk to people about what is important to them.

3. Remind them that they love to make changes and move on in two to four year cycles, and it is okay to spice things up when they get bored.

4. Don't come at them head-on, but rather stand or sit next to them to talk about an issue.

5. Recognize that they can be very volatile in their emotions, act betrayed, and become very upset. Don't be manipulated by their feelings but support them to do what's best in spite of their emotions. Remind them that passion is what drives them.

6. Enforcer-Seducers can sabotage a team effort like no other profile, so it's important to be aware that when someone is clearly not able to come out of defense, it is time to fire them or they will undermine the entire culture.

THE RULE KEEPER (KNOWLEDGEABLE ACHIEVER)

Rule Keepers are run by a tough inner critic that is always disappointed in their performance or success. They push themselves unmercifully to be perfect to the point of breakdown.

Their inner dialogue is: *I should have known better, or I should have done better.*

> *When supporting the Rule Keeper to return to their Knowledgeable Achiever:*
>
> 1. Appreciate their hard work and accomplishments, but also encourage them to do what they do best, make things work in a graceful way.
> 2. Make sure you use statistics if you are going to correct their work or try to get them to change what they are already really good at.
> 3. Ask them to help you see the big picture and how best to navigate a situation or problem.
> 4. They are very internally competitive, so ask them to beat a past record they have, and then celebrate it rather than immediately moving on to the next challenge.
> 5. Make sure you show them that what they're doing is making an important impact and is infinitely better than anyone else could do—even though they are not convinced they did it as well as could be done.

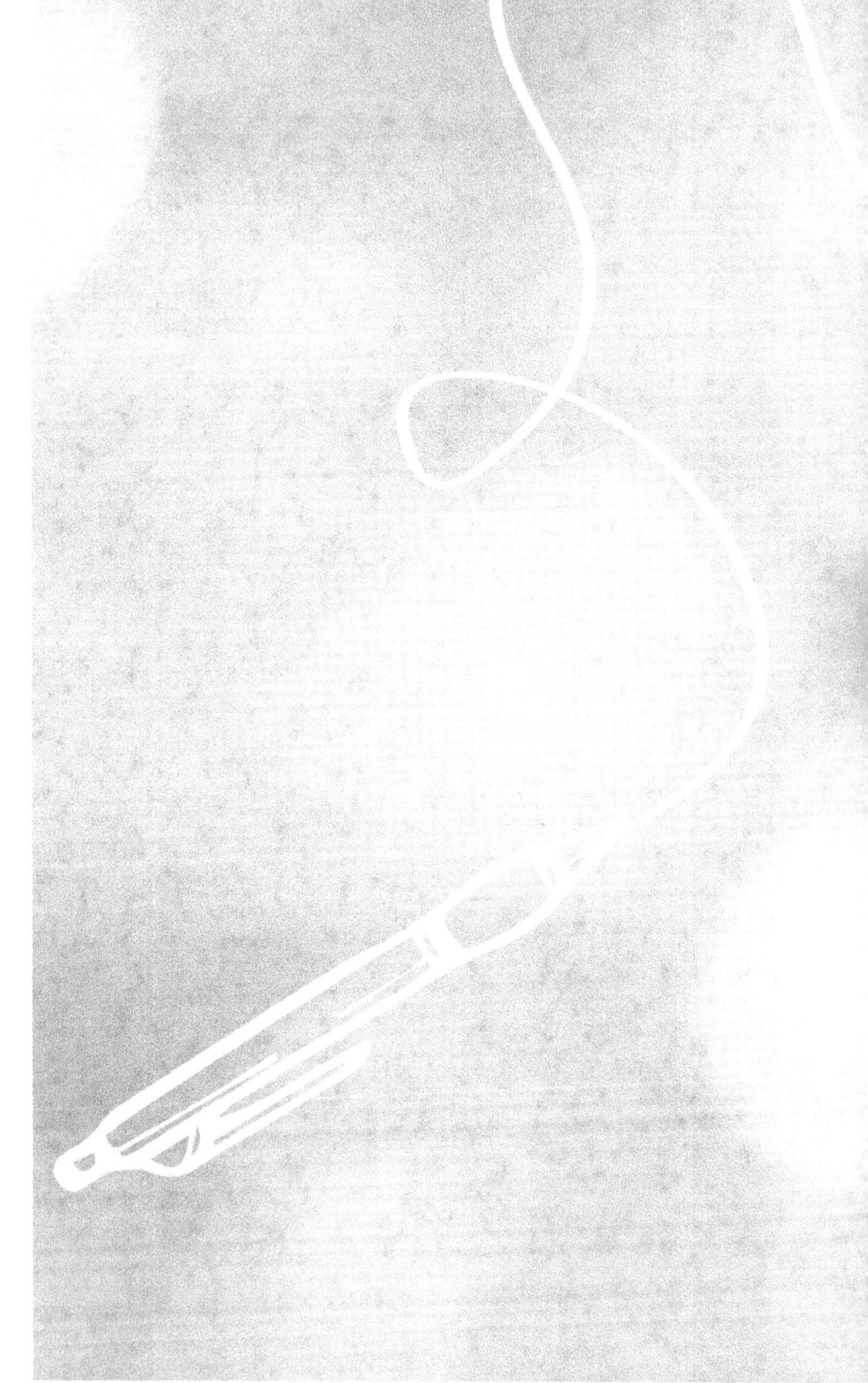

Chapter Ten
CREATE A HEALTHY CULTURE AT WORK

CHAPTER 10
CREATE A HEALTHY CULTURE AT WORK

Simply stated, a healthy workplace consists of self-aware people who know themselves and are in jobs doing what they do best. Working together as a team, they see how their unique gifts support the vision of the business. When that kind of synergy occurs, each staff member finds a way to create an atmosphere of personal and business success.

When each staff member is enjoying the perfect job for them, and has the support of management to express their core gifts and qualities, they enjoy a low-stress environment that keeps them out of their defense. They feel free to try new things because wise leaders know that making mistakes is part of growth and innovation. The result is a happier workplace and increased productivity.

Sound like paradise? It can be.

MAKE IT PERSONAL, NOT ALL BUSINESS

Whether you're a business owner or an employee, you spend a lot of time at work, often more than with your own family. But are you as close to your staff and co-workers, trusting and relying on them as you do family members?

Do they support you in giving your gifts, and help you get motivated and inspired when you're having a bad day? Or are the people you spend your days with there mainly for the money, coming to work every day just to pay the rent and put food on the table, hoping to make as much as they can and then move on? Unfortunately, most work environments fall into the second category, fostering a toxic atmosphere of stress, backbiting, and boredom. When the dollar is the bottom line, people soon leave, and any momentum for building a healthy team that works well is lost.

But when you use the Profile System at work to place people into the jobs that align with their deepest qualities and then support them to succeed, the focus shifts from a culture of *It's got to make money or it's not worth doing* to one of people giving their gifts and demonstrating their greatness.

Once you know your staff members' profiles, you can have a deeper rapport and ability to talk to them as people. People can integrate their lives with their work, not just be "all business." A colleague of mine who runs a large business with lots of employees encourages her staff to talk about what's going on outside of work in their personal lives before getting into business matters. She finds the group is closer and does better work as a result. Rule Keepers who run meetings won't always think that it's a productive use of staff time, but they need to be convinced that sharing personal experiences is one of the keys to team unity and success.

SEE THE GREATNESS

It wasn't until I shifted my view to see the greatness in each person I worked with, that I realized I don't go to work for the money. I go to work for the people I work with, and the money, quite amazingly, follows.

At my Institute of Energy Medicine, each person on my six-person team of leaders is responsible for 20 students and five staff. Leaders are all are perfectly matched based on their profiles to support the teaching objectives for all five of the profiles, not just one or two. Out of that group of over 30 staff that are needed to facilitate my weekend retreats, many also have specialties they perform after and between classes to ensure our success. Each person is very in tune with what they are able to deliver and enjoy doing, and when a need comes up in my business, I rarely have to ask for someone to take the position, because they volunteer, letting me know if I ever need anyone they can help. Together they operate as the brain of the business, connecting smoothly with each other across finely tuned synapses.

In the past, I would have been the brain, and since my brain is often forgetful and not wired like a Knowledgeable Achiever's brain, the result usually had a level of chaos. Now I have a team that is symbiotic in many ways. I give the directive, and those in each department know what to do because they are in the right position. Then, when I see the first draft of the project, it only needs a few tweaks.

This applies to the students in my programs as well. Each finds their role in the larger group dynamic when they are clear on who they are and what their gifts are. Teachers who are able to quickly assess the profiles of students can then spend their time pointing out the student's greatness, rather than trying to fix what is broken.

I feel proud of creating not only a healthy and fun work environment, but also empowering my staff to creatively make my business better every year. Another example of what a healthy workplace looks like is from a European businessman who does on a much larger scale what I've been doing and has created many highly successful businesses.

A PEOPLE-CENTERED WORK CULTURE

European-run businesses know the value of people-centered work cultures. Torben Rasmussen is the CEO of a E/Conomics, a Danish online accounting and bookkeeping service that started out with 27 people and grew to 300. Company headquarters are situated in the city of Odense, the birthplace of Hans Christian Andersen, but the story of his company's success is no fairy tale—it's real.

The company's people-centered culture is the norm in Europe, where typically workers have longer vacations and better benefits than in the U.S. But it's not only about the benefits: "We keep a better work/life balance and don't try to pack so much work in a day that people get burned-out. People enjoy themselves more at work and have less stress," he commented.

Torben's management style is unique. He prohibits big board meetings, calling together no more than three people at a time, so he can have quality contact. He takes a different desk in the building every other week, so he can train and encourage his staff wherever they are working. Once they know their job, he allows people to create their own work tasks, rather than dictating what they should do.

"The key is putting the right people in the right positions, and then getting out of their way while encouraging and supporting the best within them," he confirmed. He knows the value of giving people the freedom to be who they are and make their unique contribution. "I don't believe in organizational charts where the CEO is on top and layered below are the middle leaders and then the service people at the bottom," he said. "When you categorize people according to their job value, you keep them in a box and undervalue their true potential."

When Torben sold off some of his businesses, the new owners replaced staff mostly with people who were aggressive go-getters—Knowledgeable Achiever and Charismatic Leader-Charmer types. Consequently, the value of the business dropped considerably because the new owners didn't know how to build a healthy team through hiring the right people and then trusting and encouraging them as Torben had done. Inevitably, the turnover was higher and productivity declined.

Torben read my book, *Discover Your Purpose*, and found confirmation in the Profile System for how he runs his company: "If you know yourself and what makes you happy, and you apply that to your staff and your co-workers, it makes a big difference for everyone. Everything goes up, resulting in more loyalty and productivity."

In my Institute, I aim for a people-centered culture, and like Torben, I've found that it starts with putting the right person in the right job. Then I can support and motivate the person in ways that are tailored to fit who they are. I can then step back and count on the person to make the job their own, and that's when I can be who I am and do what I do best.

FREEDOM TO MAKE MISTAKES

What if you worked for a boss who could see your mistakes as essential to your learning? There is an urban legend that a salesman who lost five million dollars when working for IBM, went to the then CEO Tom Watson Jr. and asked if he wanted his resignation. Watson replied, "Why would I want to fire you when we've just spent $5 million training you up?"

A healthy business provides an environment where staff can make mistakes and not be crucified for them. Instead, they learn from their mistakes, knowing that the only way to improve is to take chances that may lead to failure. We are constantly making errors in life and adjusting.

It's human nature to constantly try to do new things, but if leaders communicate that people can only try new things as long as they work, they are handcuffing their staff and stifling innovation. When an employer realizes that his staff has to feel comfortable to try out new things, real innovation can occur.

The Profile System helps a person discover the qualities that most deeply fulfill them when expressed. When you hire people who are able to make decisions from that deeper place of themselves, your business thrives. When you hire someone to be who they are and then encourage that in them, they're going to make choices you wouldn't have made. But if you've placed them according to their profile, they will bring newness and transformation to your business that you could never have done.

When you work with the profiles, the idea of mistakes takes on a new meaning. The only time someone is really making a mistake is when they are trying to be someone who they are not. Failing at what you are born to do is not failure. Winning at what you have no real interest in—that is a failure.

For instance, when you put a Charismatic Leader-Charmer on your staff, you can expect that person to be aggressive, to shoot big and then leave big. That is exactly what that person's job is in life, what they are supposed to do. If you put a Knowledgeable Achiever in that position instead, you'll have someone who won't be as aggressive and will appear to make mistakes that cost the business. The Knowledgeable Achiever can't shoot from the hip. It's not what they are born to do. But a Charismatic Leader-Charmer can't not shoot from the hip. A good manager knows his or her staff's profiles and then encourages people to fulfill their potential.

Business owners spend an enormous amount of time telling people that they should be able to do things that they'll never be able to do. The people feel guilty and bad about themselves, and then fail because they are trying to do something they aren't capable of doing. When you work with the Profile System, you become clear about what a person is able to do and realize that the only mistake anyone ever makes is to try and be someone they aren't.

BUSINESS AND THE WORLD

Think about it: A business is a reflection of what is needed to create a healthy, balanced world. For the world to work, we need the five kinds of people to participate and contribute their unique gifts. We need someone to inspire and lead people, someone to run things to make it all work, someone who cares about people and makes sure their needs are met, someone with enough heart to ensure what we're doing is good for all, and finally, someone creative enough to say, *I know we've always done it this way, but here's a better way to do it, so let's keep growing and changing.*

To create a healthy, balanced culture in a business, you need leaders, achievers, feelers, caretakers, and creative thinkers. Similarly, when all five kinds of people are fully empowered to make valuable contributions to society, we get a world that works for everyone.

My student Raylene Kwasnickie, Charismatic Leader-Charmer with Team Player secondary, took what she learned at my school into her management position in corporate America. How it helped her survive and even thrive as she transformed her experience of the workplace should inspire us all.

THE POWER OF PURPOSE IN BUSINESS

RAYLENE'S STORY: MAKING A BETTER WORLD AT WORK

Raylene is a manager and software implementer in the utility industry, working for a huge company; one of the top accounting firms in the world. With a primary profile as Charismatic Leader-Charmer, her life in corporate America hasn't always been easy.

"Corporate America is an awful place to work when no one gets who you really are," Raylene commented. "It's stressful enough that they want you to do more than you're getting paid for, and even worse when they also want you to be a different person. They don't see what you could bring, so they put you in the wrong part of the organization where they try to force you to be someone you can't be."

When she started her three-year program at my Institute, Raylene's intention was to find a new career. "I figured I didn't belong in corporate America and was doing the completely wrong job. But over the course of the three-year program, I realized I had the perfect job for my profile."

Before she knew her profile, Raylene found herself often doing battle in the workplace—with herself as well as with others—and not really understanding why. Everything she did just seemed to be so hard all the time.

"As a Charismatic Leader-Charmer, I don't love structure," she reported. "But the company I work for is a very structured company, and my job implementing software needs to be very structured. If you're looking for someone on a project to

support that structure, it's never going to be me."

Understanding herself better helped Raylene to not be so hard on herself, especially over things she doesn't do well. Being aware of her profile's defense mode as Enforcer helped her to accept her battling and resistance to parts of her job.

Recently, her company was bought, and her job description changed from managing on-site project teams to managing larger internal teams, one level up from her previous responsibilities.

"Before, I could do all the work myself. But now I'm leading teams that are expected to perform, so I have to trust that people can do as good a job as I do. This is hard for me, but it's much easier when I understand their profiles and know how to motivate them."

In her new role, Raylene has to deal with technical support people, often Creative Idealists who are coding on their computers during meetings with a client. "I used to get mad," she said. "But now I tell him I need him to be in the room to answer questions, and after I get the answer, he can go back to what he was doing." Displaying her profile's strength, she now expresses the assertiveness of a Charismatic Leader-Charmer instead of the battling resistance of an Enforcer.

Could the Profile System be used inside such a giant corporation like the one Raylene works for to make a better working world for all? It's the kind of culture many companies say they want, and so as more people enter and stay in corporate America with knowledge of their life purpose, an acceptance of others' differences, and skills to manage people based on their profiles, it's very likely what we are going to see!

Conclusion
Where To Start in Your Business or Workplace

CONCLUSION
WHERE TO START IN YOUR BUSINESS OR WORKPLACE

HERE IS A CHECKLIST TO GET YOU STARTED IN USING THE POWER OF PURPOSE IN BUSINESS TO MASTER YOUR BUSINESS WORLD:

1. *Start with you:* Know your Big Why and discover your business purpose through the Life Purpose Profile System. Learn about what motivates you, and what to expect when you are under stress and go into defensive patterns of behavior.

2. Find out what it is that you, and you alone, deliver based on your profile, and learn how best to deliver that unique quality in your business or work.

3. Choose your perfect career, profession or business based on your knowledge of the profiles.

4. Know who your customer and clients are and how to make them happy so they'll keep coming back.

5. Match your marketing/branding to who you really are.

6. Nip problems in the bud before disaster strikes by knowing how to relate to all 5 profiles in their uniqueness.

7. When building a staff, hire from candidates' profiles, not their resumes alone, to create a productive workplace where everyone is happy and successful in what they do.

8. Use the Profile System to motivate and manage your staff, and fulfill their unique needs.

9. Train your staff to know their own Life Purpose Profile and also the profiles of those they work with, so they can support other team members' success.

10. Have fun!

If you want to find out more about the many courses, events, assessments and products available at the Rhys Thomas Institute of Energy Medicine, go to www.rhysthomasinstitute.com to find out more.

APPENDIX A
CHART: HOW TO QUICKLY READ THE PROFILE OF ANYONE

CREATIVE IDEALIST (THINKER)

Initial Impression: When encountering a Creative Idealist, you'll notice they either have a nervous energy or appear lost in thought, even when having their photo taken. You will often see a head tilt, indicating how the mind and body are disconnected and frequently in different worlds.

Eye Contact: There is a general fear in the eyes, especially if you are too direct with them. Otherwise, Creative Idealists have larger than normal eyes that appear to be daydreaming.

Body Observations: Creative Idealists are usually thin and can be very tall; the man shown in the picture to the right is six foot five. They can be overweight but not have a heavy personal presence. They may appear disjointed (i.e., one part of the body bigger than the other), and as if front/back, top/bottom, right/left are parts that don't seem to go together.

Energy Observations: They have fragmented energy and focus, and can appear flaky or spacey. They can be stiff at the core, and have bands of tight energy at the waist, diaphragm, and the throat that block aggression from rising up through the body to be expressed. Energy is often blocked at the base of the skull, giving them the appearance of being split, head from body. They are internally motivated and stay inside their heads most of the time, not often noticing what is going on around them.

THE POWER OF PURPOSE IN BUSINESS

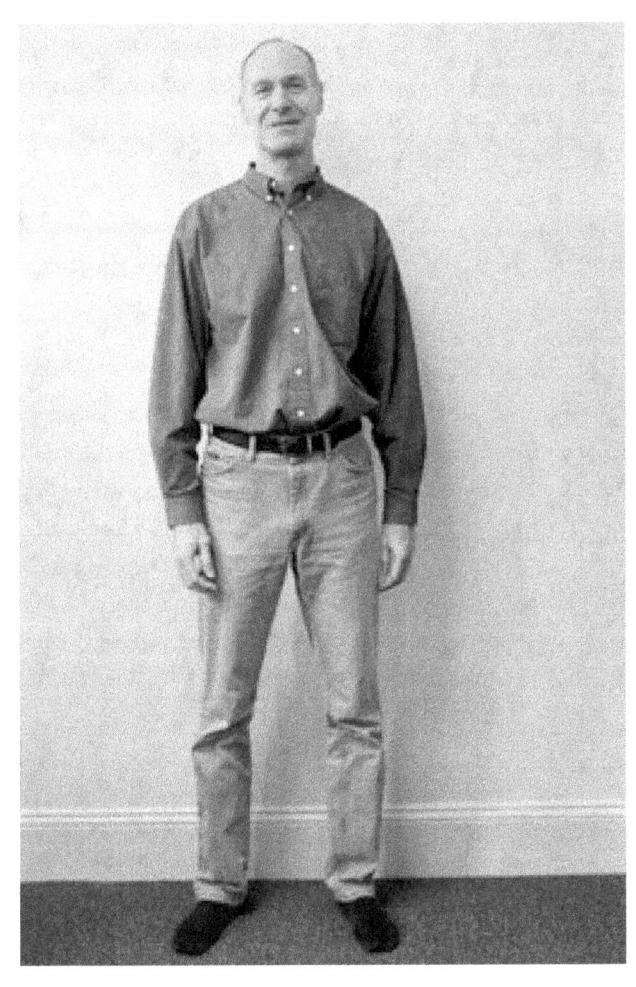

EMOTIONAL INTELLIGENCE SPECIALIST (POOR ME)

Initial Impression: When meeting an Emotional Intelligence Specialist, you will notice their gentle, almost innocent quality. Their body tends to be soft and flexible, not defined or muscular, and the face is often childlike in its openness. They are grounded through their deep feelings and emotions, and through deep connection and empathy for others.

Eye Contact: Emotional Intelligence Specialists have large, puppy-dog eyes that are deep and compassionate but can seem needy for deeper connection. Eyes are often watery, since Emotional Intelligence Specialists are never far from crying with either joy or pain in any moment.

Body Observations: Their body is generally thin and soft with muscles that are unformed or depleted in some way. There is a concave chest, the shoulders slump forward, and there is a collapsed feeling where the body bends at the bottom of the ribs. They often have a little belly and pronounced curvature in the lower back.

Energy Observations: The energy level for Emotional Intelligence Specialists is low, pooled in the hips and heart area, which are both energetic centers of emotion. They appear not very grounded due to avoiding their many feelings by talking about their feelings instead of letting their feelings build into positive action. They look and feel feminine and/or childlike, and in their defense mode as Poor Me, you will feel them as empty, clinging, and dependent. They are internally motivated, letting their own feelings always be their guide.

THE POWER OF PURPOSE IN BUSINESS

www.RhysMethod.com | www.RhysThomasInstitute.com

TEAM PLAYER (PEOPLE PLEASER)

Initial Impression: When encountering a Team Player, they will seem warm and inviting. They give great hugs and have broad, open faces, smiling easily when they greet you. These people have huge hearts, giving you the feeling they are there for you, even more than they are for themselves.

Eye Contact: Team Players will look directly into your eyes when talking with you, their gaze rarely straying, showing how much they are connected and care about you.

Body Observations: They are often heavy and stocky, carrying extra weight in the belly area. Their neck can be compacted with rounded shoulders. There is an overall muscle-bound quality indicative of great strength but little agility. They have great endurance for heavy work.

Energy Observations: Team Players carry their energy in the belly and heart areas. Their energy is grounded through their legs with big calves not for sprinting but for heavy lifting and holding still. This blocks upward movement energetically, so Team Players often feel trapped and not free in their lives to do whatever they want. They are externally motivated, and feel more of what you are feeling than what they are feeling.

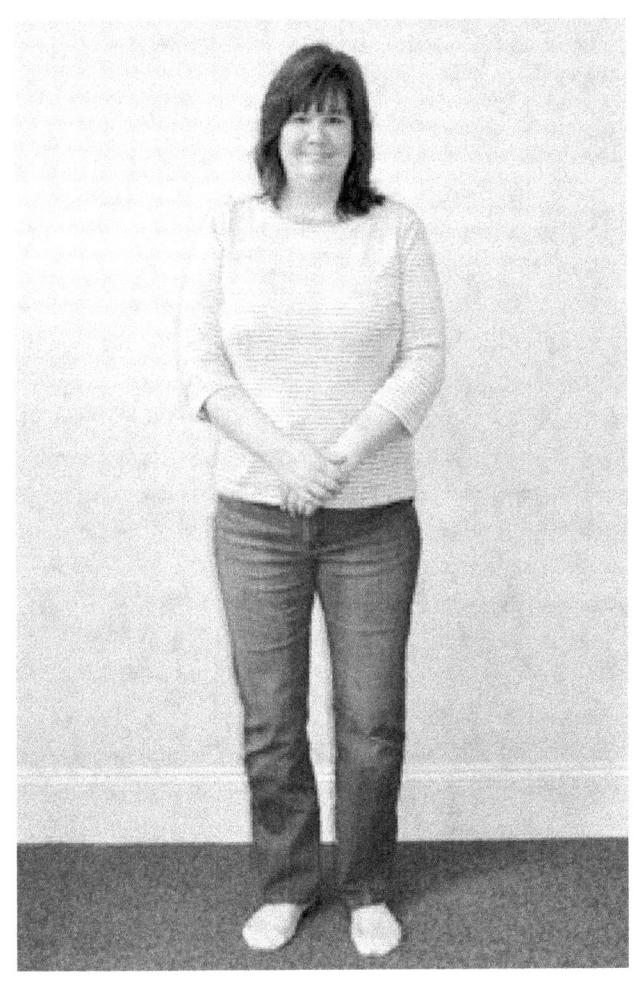

APPENDIX A

CHARISMATIC LEADER-CHARMER (ENFORCER-SEDUCER)

Initial Impression: When encountering a Charismatic Leader-Charmer, you will notice a dynamic energy that is at times magnetically attracting. They are eye-catching in appearance, even if not classically beautiful (which they often are) and can be sensually seductive and alluring. Their most salient traits are their fearlessness and sensuality, and their ability to inspire you just by being around them.

Eye Contact: The Charismatic Leader-Charmer has a direct piercing eye gaze that makes sure you are paying attention and are trustworthy. Or their eyes may shift or glare as they dodge questions about their situation that might reveal more of their personal issues or vulnerability.

Body Observations: They generally have two distinct body types. The strong, heavy-set, body type is very powerful and generally has a life focused on protection of others (strong Team Player secondary). Or they will have the more sexually attractive hourglass body with thin waist and broad shoulders and chest. This type will be more generally charismatic, seductive, illusive, and narcissistic in their life choices (strong Emotional Intelligence Specialist secondary). Their skin and musculature often has an elastic quality, allowing them to go from being out of shape to in shape in a matter of weeks.

Energy Observations: The Charismatic Leader-Charmer has the most energy of the five profiles. No matter what size body they have, they are always stronger than they appear, and are capable of extreme physical and emotional swings. They hold most of their energy in their head, shoulders, and neck (where they always have tension), and arms, areas that tend to be muscular and strong. This concentration of energy supports their tendency to use words, as well as face, eyes and hands to inspire, control, and pressure others. They are externally focused, since they are warriors at heart and need to manage the energy field and those in it.

THE POWER OF PURPOSE IN BUSINESS

KNOWLEDGEABLE ACHIEVER (RULE KEEPER)

Initial Impression: When meeting a Knowledgeable Achiever, you'll notice their often perfect posture and an evenly balanced energy. They are proud of their bodies, displaying a self-confidence you can feel. Their most salient trait is their ability to manage their energy internally, making you feel safe in their presence.

Eye Contact: Knowledgeable Achievers look you straight in the eye and are not afraid of you looking as directly back at them. In defense, they will assess you with their eyes, judging and processing the things you say and do. When you speak to them about new ideas, you may see skepticism in their eyes or a politeness while they wait for you to finish so they can share their own thoughts on the matter.

Body Observations: They are usually fit, evenly proportioned, and attractive. They tend to be physically coordinated and rarely carry extra fat on their bodies. Good posture, well-groomed. Usually strong and athletic, but having tight muscles, especially in the lower back. They are often well-grounded with good balance.

Energy Observations: Knowledgeable Achievers have a very balanced energy. They often feel emotionally rigid, but hiding behind the often strong chest is a delicate heart that when touched can melt their tough inner critic. They command your attention with strong and well-organized thoughts and ideas. Their bodies are contained and internally driven to be the best they can be.

THE POWER OF PURPOSE IN BUSINESS

APPENDIX B
WORKSHEET: QUICKLY READ THE PROFILE OF ANYONE YOU DO BUSINESS WITH

Use this worksheet to quickly assess a person you relate to at work or in your business, including customers, clients, employees, supervisor, co-workers, potential hires, etc. Refer to the previous section for more details in each category.

Name and Business Relationship: _____

_____

1. Body Observation: Which of the profile body types do they have? (check one)

    Creative Idealist/Thinker

    Emotional Intelligence Specialist/Poor Me

    Team Player/People Pleaser

    Knowledgeable Achiever/Rule Keeper

    Charismatic Leader-Charmer/Enforcer-Seducer

2. Eye Contact: What is the quality of their eye contact? (check one)

    Anxious/thoughtful/nobody home. (Creative Idealist)

    Needy/loving/deep and soft. (Emotional Intelligence Specialist)

    Attentive/caring/solid. (Team Player)

    Shifting/seductive/charming/piercing. (Charismatic Leader-Charmer)

    Critical/confident/assessing you. (Knowledgeable Achiever)

3. Energy Observation: What is their energy management?
   (check one)

   Out of body, avoidant, energy moving up but not grounded, expanded through ideas. (Creative Idealist)

   Soft and melting/emotional/non-threatening/childlike/ easily overwhelmed by others' emotions. (Emotional Intelligence Specialist)

   Warm/ big heart/hugging/focused totally on you. (Team Player)

   Big energy/tricky/hard to read/energy shifts depending on the topic-situation/volatile emotions are up or down, crazy or controlled/poor boundaries/ overwhelming.
   (Charismatic Leader-Charmer)

   Grounded/contained/ balanced or withheld energy/not much emotion/great boundaries/attention. (Knowledgeable Achiever)

4. Primary/Secondary Profile: From your assessment, what is their primary profile? Secondary profile? (Use "1" for primary, "2" for secondary.)

   Creative Idealist/Thinker

   Emotional Intelligence Specialist/Poor Me

   Team Player/People Pleaser

   Knowledgeable Achiever/Rule Keeper

   Charismatic Leader-Charmer/Enforcer-Seducer

APPENDIX B

5. Profile Defense: Which defense do they use the most? Who do they pretend they are that you cannot feel? (check one)

   Thinker: Mentally spinning/spacing out (Creative Idealist)

   Poor Me: Overly sensitive/ overwhelmed/tired.
   (Emotional Intelligence Specialist)

   People Pleaser: Can't say no/selfless (Team Player)

   Enforcer-Seducer: Controlling /seducer/manipulator
   (Charismatic Leader-Charmer)

   Rule Keeper: Rigid/perfectionist/inner critic
   (Knowledgeable Achiever)

6. Deeper Exploration: Use this space to explore actions and decisions when doing business with this person, based on your knowledge of their profile.

   For example:

   What do you feel is the core strength of their primary profile?

   _____

   _____

   _____

   _____

   What kind of position would you best place them in?

   _____

   _____

   _____

   _____

How would you best support or motivate this person?
___
___
___
___

What could you expect with working with or for this person?
___
___
___
___

What is the best marketing strategy to use with this person?
___
___
___
___

ABOUT THE AUTHOR
Rhys Thomas

Rhys Thomas is a visionary author, speaker, and trainer in the energy medicine field. He is celebrated worldwide as a pioneer in energy medicine due to his synthesis and reinterpretation of energy medicine techniques for personal and professional transformation. He is the author of *Discover Your Purpose*, the creator of the Rhys Method® transformational system and the Rhys Method® coaching programs, taught exclusively at the Rhys Thomas Institute of Energy Medicine and in his online trainings.

When he was 38, Rhys had an awakening experience that ended fifteen years of killing himself slowly as a workaholic. He had the realization that even though he was successful on the outside, he was living what he called "a quiet desperation" in his life. He was trying to be someone he was not, running three businesses at once in hopes of getting ahead but missing his life in the process.

The catalyst for his awakening was studying energy medicine and a profound realization that his internal world had to come first if he was to truly live and share his true purpose before it was too late. Finding his purpose in this way led to his starting a totally different business and life practices that today serve both his highest good as well as the good of those he works with and his clients.

From his awakening, Rhys could see that he was not alone. He discovered that the source of people's pain and their frustration in their careers was based in trying to be and do what society and culture told them they were supposed do. Causing them to do work that ultimately drained them of their enthusiasm for life.

As a teacher, Rhys developed an easily learned system of self-understanding called the Rhys Method® Life Purpose Profile System that moves far beyond any other current system of self-awareness and guidance. Rhys has impacted people around the globe through his videos, speaking events, programs, and his Institute.

With *The Power of Purpose in Business,* he aims to equally impact how people do business, using this same knowledge to free people to bring forward their truest gifts in life and find both internal and external success and happiness.

Learn more and connect with Rhys at:

www.RhysThomasInstitute.com

Facebook: Facebook.com/rhysthomasinstitute/

Twitter: Twitter.com/rtiem

e-mail: support@rhysthomasinstitute.com